A Project of TRT Ministries

P.M.S. FACTOR (POWER, MONEY & SEX)

P.M.S. FACTOR (POWER, MONEY & SEX)

Scripture quotations marked KJV are taken from the King James Version of the Bible.

Scripture is taken from GOD'S WORD®, © 1995 God's Word to the Nations. Used by permission of Baker Publishing Group.

Power, Money & Sex (P.M.S.)
ISBN
Copyright© 2014 by Tommy R. Twitty
Tommy R. Twitty Ministries
P.O. Box 613
Chesnee, SC 29323

Library of Congress Control Number: **2014913099**

P.M.S. FACTOR (POWER, MONEY & SEX)

Introduction

The P.M.S. Factor is based upon the total relationship between a man and a woman, which was God's original blueprint and foundation from the beginning. Such relationships are based on three factors: Power, Money, and Sex.

The Power Factor:

For this book, the term power refers to the kind of power that can become abusive, controlling, dictatorial, and overly demanding. Within a relationship, either the man or the woman can become abusive or controlling. This happened between Jezebel and Ahab; Jezebel simply refused to co-exist in a balanced, intimate, mutually understanding partnership of intimacy. In these situations, one individual seeks or desires power in that relationship. Two types of experiences in life can characterize a man or woman's desire for control, obsessive-passion, domineering nature, and/or dominating tendencies. One such experience is when something has happened in a past relationship that has left the person feeling broken, rejected, bitter, and full of resentment. These incidents may be rooted in a previous marriage, divorce, engagement, or dating relationship where they experienced domestic violence, physical, mental, verbal, or perhaps even spiritual abuse. And, now that the relationship has ended and the individual is seeking a new relationship, it may become evident that he or she has taken on the Jezebel spirit, as a result of being cheated on and hurt. Now this person is looking for a safe relationship with someone who can be controlled, dominated, influenced, or overpowered. This is a protective shield against ever being hurt again. The individual begins to erect firewalls and defense mechanisms, resulting in being on the defensive, with a need or desire to ultimately control the relationship and to have all of the power.

The Money Factor:

Money is the answer to all things. Eccl 10:9b KJV says, "A feast is made for laughter, and wine maketh merry: but money answers all things." Proverbs 10:15 NKJV says, "The rich man's wealth is his strong city: the destruction of the poor is their poverty."

In Genesis, you will discover that before God instituted marriage, or ordained man and woman to be one, He had already made provisions. He had created everything that Adam and Eve would have ever needed in Paradise. They would never have a want, or a need for financial stability.

The Bible says that God created four rivers (Gen 2:9-15NKJV); in verse fifteen, the first river was the Pishon, second was the Gihon, third was the Hiddekel, and the fourth was the Euphrates. It was always God's intention for man to have four sources of income or revenue to sustain them. As you read this book, you will discover that a relationship with no vision for generating provision will create an instability in consistency for generating future wealth, because it's hard to have romance without finance. In the chapters referencing the money factor, you will be able to identify reasons for the impression that a majority of separations and divorces are related to or because of money problems.

P.M.S. FACTOR (POWER, MONEY & SEX)

The Sex Factor:

In Gen 4:1 ERV **vs.** Gen. 29:23 ERV, the Bible says, "Adam had sexual relations with his wife Eve. She became pregnant and gave birth to a son. She named him Cain. Eve said, "With the Lord's help, I have made a man!" In Gen 29:23 ERV it says, "That night Laban brought his daughter Leah to Jacob. Jacob and Leah had **sexual relations together**." In the chapters dealing with sexual relationships, you will discover that in Genesis 4, this was a relationship ordained by God and in Genesis 29 the relationship of Jacob and Leah was a relationship ordained by man. A relationship that is ordained and brought together by God brings mutual fulfillment and oneness in the **Four Love Level Connections,** which will be discussed later in this book.

The four connections, in order, are the Spiritual Love Level Connection, the Physical Love Level Connection, the Emotional Love Level Connection, and the Mental Love Level Connection.

The Spiritual Love Level Connection is about sharing a 20/20 vision together, having a strategy, purpose, goals, and covenant in regard to beliefs. The Physical Love Level Connection is where you share with one another your physical capacities. Do you know and understand your partner's physical issues or medical needs? Do you have life and medical insurance right now or will you be getting it? Is your partner unhealthy or accident prone? These are things you should know before you marry or enter into marriage; whether illnesses exists, or whether the other person lacks the ability to bring in income due to their physical abilities. It's hard to share your vision when you desire a two story home, but have trailer-home money.

P.M.S. FACTOR (POWER, MONEY & SEX)

The next thing that you should do is to name your priorities. Do you want to have a home first or children first? What is the order of your goals; what comes first? In a relationship, you will need to understand the debt to income ratio. If you have debt, what is your plan for canceling the debt? Will your mortgage be 30 years or 15 years? Will your car loan be five or three years in duration? Will you have two kids or five kids?

In addition, with the physical connection you must talk about living arrangements. Where will you live; in what state or city? Will you live in an urban neighborhood or in the country? Are you looking to rent or buy a three-bedroom or a one-bedroom home or apartment? As part of the physical connection, you will have to know the extent of your sexual drive and your partner's sexual drive. Are you very active or inactive? Are you conservative or are you spontaneous and extreme? Are you prepared if something happens? Will you leave your partner in debt or will they be able to enjoy life?

The Emotional Love Level Connection deals with the depth of the relationship before saying "I do". What is the temperament of each person in the relationship? Take maturity level, behavior, character, and confidence levels into account. What is each person's state of mind and what is the extent of his or her ability to handle problems under pressure? How does each handle controversy, bad news, or disappointment? Is your partner the type of person who confronts a crisis with the ability to communicate, or will he or she run and shut down?

The Mental Love Level Connection is concerned with the mind. How does the individual handle rejection when you try to talk about concerns or something that is objectionable? When you approach these topics, does your partner become argumentative, out of control, violent, abusive, or controlling, taking on the form of a dictator or a destructive personality? Is the person passive? Is your partner immature? When trouble comes, does the person run away or go back to their Mother?

It's important to know that the person you are with is mentally stable; it's even more important than spiritual stability, because a person that is mentally broken has been attacked by ungodly soul-ties. It's good to have three of the Love Levels, but without an understanding on the mental level, the rest will fall apart because without mental stability, you can fall into a season of spiritual despair. You can enter into a season of your relationship where you lose the cohesiveness and the sexual chemistry. Emotionally, you enter into a season where your relationship is full of disagreement and arguments. But it takes the fourth level, the Emotional Love Level Connection, to create soundness and balance when you are struggling as lovers. Understanding this connection will allow you to remain as friends. The Bible says, "Faithful are the wounds of a friend; (Prov 27:6a), because sometimes lovers become enemies, but real friends become more loyal." This is why, in any successful relationship, you must be friends before you become lovers. This is why, once you have brought closure to one relationship, you never start a new relationship until you are completely mentally, physically, socially, and spiritually healed from what the previous relationship has done to you.

P.M.S. FACTOR (POWER, MONEY & SEX)

Table of Contents

Chapter 1

Single, but not Alone

God's Original Blueprint for man and woman in the State of Singleness
(Gen 2:7-8; 15-18; 20-24 AMP)

God's original blueprint for man and woman in the state of singleness was to first reveal unto the man and woman their identities. The first thing that God did for man was to form him out of the dust of the ground, and He then shaped him into his own image (Scripture - Gen 1:26-27).

The second thing God did was to take the man that He had formed in his image and make him into his likeness. The third thing he did was to breathe into man's nostrils, making man a living soul. The word form represented man's negative image, but after He formed man's image, He then created man into His likeness. The likeness is the proof or the positive of man. This process is similar to a camera that opens its lens and uses its shutter to take a picture. The flash goes off to illuminate and capture the negative image of an individual and bring it back. With the closing of the shutter, the lens allows for the captured image to be placed on the film. Then the photographer takes the negative film into the dark room and develops it into the positive (the proof), or into the likeness of what we see.

Then, the Bible says that God planted a garden called Eden for the man. A place full of delight, pleasure, and fulfillment: "the spot'. He gave man a new responsibility, and with this new responsibility, God gave man dominion, power, and authority over the earth so that man would subdue it, be fruitful, multiply, and increase.

Then God gave man a ministry and an assignment. This is the point where God took everything that He had ever created and placed man over it, to manage it and to be steward over it. Next, we find that God began to have a conference call in the heavens, or He literally spoke to those in the heavens, to say that it is not good for man to be alone. Man was single, but not lonely. He then brought all of the animals to man to see what man would name them, but for Adam, there was no companion (Gen. 2:18a).

He put Adam to sleep, and took woman from man's side or rib. He presented the woman to the man. This is the point when Adam describes her as "bone of my bone and flesh of my flesh" (Gen. 2:21-23).

Single means to be whole, mature, and complete. It also means oneness. This is why the Bible says that when Adam and Eve came together, they became one, not two (Gen. 2: 24). This simply means that they became Godly soul-mates. The union of a man and a woman does not make them whole, because if the male or female does not come into the relationship whole as an individual, then being in a relationship will not make them whole or make them one.

Man and woman become one because they take on equality in sharing the same vision, the same responsibility, the same assignment, and the same destiny. This is because the same responsibility God gave Adam in the beginning is now the same responsibility placed on Eve. It's only when the relationship no longer experiences equality, but division, that a God-ordained relationship becomes divided. In Mark 3:25, the Bible says, A house that is divided against itself, that house cannot stand." When Eve lost focus in regard to her responsibility and assignment, she caused a division within the house. The reason she lost focus and became distracted was that she began to seek out more power and influence from Satan, the serpent, who deceived her. Romans 12:3 says "For I say, through the grace given to me, to every man that is among you, not to think of himself more highly than he ought to think..." It was when Eve thought of herself more highly then she ought to, seeking out more power, that she ate from the forbidden tree. It was her need for power that brought destruction to her relationship and caused her to lose focus in fulfilling her assignment.

God, unlike man, started with nothing, but He saw the potential. A relationship is a process, and in the beginning it may look like nothing, but God knows the potential of man choosing his helpmeet. In this process, called a relationship, you will continue to see the negative image of man until you remember the uniqueness, or the likeness of God, that you know is within that person. When you're connected to the right person, the two of you become what wasn't, because you always had the potential to become what you are supposed to be. However, you needed the one who understood your uniqueness and likeness to help you discover who you are as individuals and as a couple.

The first gift God gave to man was Himself; you will never understand yourself until you've been with someone that understands you better than you do. The person that you are meant to be with understands your uniqueness, even when there is nothing going on.

The second gift God gave man was His presence, in the Garden of Eden; Eden was a gift to man. Earlier, we identified something that was called "the spot", and to bring further clarity, we want you to consider Eden as "the spot". As long as you stay in that spot, no weapon formed against you will prosper. In that spot, you will experience moments. Moments are times when we experience God's favor and blessings. As long as we stay in the spot, we will continue to be in the presence of God.

P.M.S. FACTOR (POWER, MONEY & SEX)

Let's take a moment to explain the meaning of God's "work" for man. God commanded man to do work, and before Adam would ever know Eve, he understood that man was to work."Work" is different from a job, where you go and receive training for a particular skill, and then perform this skill at someone else's place of business. Work from God is our ministry or business. It is our ability to produce or to provide for those God has entrusted in our care. God intended for man to work for himself, to work the gift which God gave him with authority, dominion, and power. The "work" that God gave us is what we were born to do, and even when you die the work goes on. This is the double portion; your heirs reap the benefits of your work.

God planted Adam in the Garden of Eden, which He had made for him. In the Garden, He planted provisions, with one stipulation. In Genesis 2:16-17 NKJV, He tells Adam that he may freely eat of every tree in the garden, except for the tree of the knowledge of good and evil. He was not to eat of this tree, and if he did, he would surely die.

In the Garden, the ground worked for Adam to produce what he wanted and what he saw a need for.

P.M.S. FACTOR (POWER, MONEY & SEX)

When you "work", the ground will always work for you, and when you have a job, you will always work for the ground. With this understanding, man is successful in the Garden and in his relationship with God. Man recognizes that he is in "the spot"; he knows God's presence, the gifts given to him by God, he understands the culture of God, he understands the environment, and he understands how to be blessed, how to be fruitful. It's only when a man does not understand these things that he should be alone.

What godly woman wants a man who does not know his purpose? A real man only needs a helpmeet when he knows who he is. God brought animals to man, so that man could choose his helpmeet. Adam named every animal, but they were not suitable for man, so Adam waited for his helpmeet, and while he waited, he kept doing ministry.

In Genesis 2:21-22KJV, God does surgery on the man, and out of man, he birthed woman. She was not formed like man was formed, but she was birthed out of man, or made from man. Woman comes from the weaker side of man, the side where his heart is. When God made her, He made her with curves, because He knew that man was the foundation, but woman was the structure of man and was made for his foundation.

We all know that man is the head, and this comes from the fact that man is the foundation, but every great builder understands that no structure can stand unless it has a good foundation, a firm foundation. So what does this mean for relationships? The enemy, Satan, is after the foundation. He wants man because a structure can't stand without a foundation.

When you remove a man from a relationship with a woman, God's structure for man begins to fall. Woman was created to cover man's heart. She is affectionate and detailed, but she is not the foundation. She must understand that men are not interested in feelings all the time, but to build a relationship, she must know how to cover her foundation. No man wants to hear all the details from a woman without having his needs met first. In a relationship, a man must fulfill the **"Five P Factors"**

1. Priest: Man must cover his house and minister to his family.

2. Prophet: Man must point the way, or the direction, in which his household is going.

3. Protector: Man must protect his home.

4. Provider: It is man's responsibility to bring provisions to his home.

5. Pleaser: It is man's responsibility to please those in his home, but it was not until Eve pleased Adam that he was able to fulfill all of his responsibilities. For this reason, God created male and female.

The word man is considered spiritual, while male is considered flesh, just as woman is considered spiritual and female flesh. A male has sexual factors or desires, and females are more affectionate, but until a woman learns how to fulfill the sexual desires of her man, she will continue to have affections, and a man that will not be able to listen.

Relationships are a strategic part of the kingdom, and it was never intended for man to be with a number of females; it was always purposed for him to find his wife. Although they are two individuals and single, the two shall become one. When two come into an agreement or relationship, a covenant is always established, and to establish a covenant, blood must be shed and this is why women bleed when they have sex for the first time. This is why they were to marry before having sex. Having sex was to be a sign of their confession and agreement to establish a covenant. Proverbs 18:22 NKJV, says that when a man finds a wife, he finds a good thing and obtains favor. His wife is presented to him by God as being the one chosen by the Father. When God presents the woman, they are back in "the spot". If you can imagine, Adam is awake and he sees two people coming toward him. He recognizes the woman and says this is bone of my bone, flesh of my flesh. It is this relationship that God originally planned. It is this relationship that He favors. In Proverbs, the word "finds" means that when a man discerns his wife, when he sees her, he will know her and understand her. He will understand her hurt and her pain. This is why he can call her his bone. It's important to note that when a man finds his wife, he immediately obtains favor. Everything becomes fruitful and multiplies. He realizes his vision and purpose.

So what caused this oneness to be broken? Adam and Eve shared their honeymoon suite (Eden) with a snake. They let someone come in who should have never been allowed to speak over, speak in, or speak to their relationship. Man and woman became vulnerable, and they strayed from the presence of God. They left "the spot". You can lose everything when you leave the presence of God and any man out of the presence of God will find it hard to fulfill a woman, because he will not know his purpose.

Chapter 2

Who's Blaming Whom?

We may be maturing spiritually, but naturally we have not obtained the fulfillment of a Godly relationship, and the enemy is still after everyone's home.

Many people have nice appliances and have invested a great deal in them and in themselves, but what and where we have failed is in knowing that these things don't work without power. We don't work without power, and many believers have strayed away from their power source, only to find themselves starting to fizzle out like a light bulb that is about to blow.

To better deal with this issue of who's blaming whom, let's remember what happened. In Genesis Chapter Three, the Bible starts out by telling us how cunning the serpent is. It even indicates that he is the most cunning of all the beasts of the field.

The first thing the serpent does is to tempt the woman, by asking her to question what God has told her not to do. But even more than questioning God, she liked the idea that she would become wiser,

P.M.S. FACTOR (POWER, MONEY & SEX)

smarter, and that she would have power. When you try to be more than what God planned for you to be, you will begin to operate outside of the will of God. To some degree, we all crave power, but many of us have unplugged ourselves from the power source. Eve wanted more power and when she saw the fruit to be good, she ate, and then she gave it to her husband. Adam was with Eve, when she took of the fruit; he was not off somewhere in another part of the garden. Adam was in the house while Eve was talking to the snake. He was right there when the mistake was made.

> Gen 6:6 ERV: The woman could see that the tree was beautiful and the fruit looked so good to eat. *She also liked the idea that it would make her wise.* So she took some of the fruit from the tree and ate it. *Her husband was there with her,* so she gave him some of the fruit, and he ate it.

So, who's blaming whom? You can't resolve anything when you are still placing blame. In verses 10-13, blame is passed on from the man to the woman, and from the woman to the serpent. But before we can get to who's blaming whom and those who want power, let's figure out how we got here. Let's take some natural things into consideration, as well as some spiritual things. This chapter will apply to everyone, unless you're choosing to be celibate, or to abstain from relationships.

Let's use what we call the **"Four Love Level Connections"**. These connections determine how we all come together, or are drawn together, to develop relationships. Before you can enter into any relationship, you need to connect on all levels.

<u>Love Level Connection #1:</u> The *Spiritual Connection* is the least of all the connections. It is a good thing for one believer to marry another believer, but it is not necessarily an indication of the right connection. The union of two believers does not mean that two positive people are getting together, or that they will have a wonderful relationship. At this level, a couple should know one another's beliefs; they should agree on the doctrine under which they have chosen to come in covenant; and they should share vision, strategy, beliefs, purpose, goals, and covering. Additionally, they must understand the impact of falling for someone just because both go to church regularly. Each needs to know God individually.

It's also necessary to have the ability to recognize someone who may attempt to exert spiritual power within the relationship. Many believers may not recognize or notice spiritual abuse, but someone who believes that they have an authority based on God's word may attempt to use this power to manipulate or control his or her mate. No one has the right to feel that they are more right, more holy, or more righteous than anyone else. At this level, two believers should have established a commitment to serve God, but how and where must be determined. They should consider their spiritual goals and what ministry God has given them as individuals. You can't develop a good relationship with God and one another without knowing what each has been gifted by God to do.

Love Level Connection #2: The *physical or natural connection*. This connection requires that the two individuals determine where they are physically and financially. During the courting period, or when individuals are considering a relationship, this may be the most important connection component to be discussed. At this level, the couple should ask themselves questions, such as who will perform tasks in the home. Will one person work and the other stay at home?

When you discuss with your mate both the physical and the spiritual connections, the spiritual cannot

P.M.S. FACTOR (POWER, MONEY & SEX)

outweigh the natural. For example, you may be ambitious in worship and serving God, but bringing home $10,000 a year is not enough to pay for a $100,000 home. You need to determine your short-term and long-term goals. Do not use this level to spiritualize things that need to happen in the natural. Determine who has debt and how you will eliminate that debt. "Don't try to live big when little got you."

Couples considering making a connection should know what kind of income will be coming in, or how much income they will need to live the lifestyle to which they are accustomed. Some of this may seem elementary, but it's real when it comes to having a good relationship.

Each needs to know what the other feels, thinks, and believes about a number of things, including living arrangements. A clean person can't live with someone who is dirty. A couple who have been dating away from the home, or at restaurants, and then decides to invite their mate back to their home, can lose their relationship if their mate discovers that the individual is messy or unclean. These things may seem minor, but when you decide to get into a relationship with someone, you need to know. You need to know their medical history and their life expectancy, because you may be a person who does not want to end up having to physically take care of the other. In a relationship, we have to connect on these things.

Something else you should consider when dating is insurance. If you're planning on marrying someone and they have a lot of debt, what will you do if something happens? Can the spouse pay off the debt or will they be left miserable and in debt? You need to know who this person is if you plan on being with him or her for the rest of your life.

In relationships you need to be naked and not ashamed. Don't try to overlook what you see as a one-time thing. Ask the question, because the individual may surprise you when they say that's how they are. Some people let things go on in their relationships for so long that they don't know how to talk about them. It's even more important that the people of God deal with these connections. Identifying where you are and who you are in these connections will help those who plan to marry, as well as those who are already married. If we are honest with ourselves, we would wish that someone would have told us these things before getting into a marriage. If we had asked our mates and spouses how they felt about these things before getting married, many couples probably would not be together now.

Let's consider one more thing in regard to physical connections, and let's keep it real. God gave the insight to bring forth this word and to document this P.M.S. (Power, Money, and Sex) series, so let's talk about sex. Ask your mate what he or she expects when it comes to having sex, and how often they expect to have it, and know that this question is for everyone, not just young couples. What about those who have been married for a period of time? Does your mate feel that his or her sexual needs are being met, or has he or she started looking elsewhere?

Do married couples struggle with having sex because they are married? And if you are still dating, do you plan to have children right away, because having sex frequently increases the possibility of having children sooner rather than later? What pleases your mate? What does he or she expect in the bedroom? Because whether you are both believers or not, many understand that the bedroom is undefiled, but if you don't deal with these sexual needs, you are creating a sex-trap.

P.M.S. FACTOR (POWER, MONEY & SEX)

If we do not deal with these things from a Godly perspective, then the world is left to make their own interpretation from what they believe they know. So it's important that the church deal with these issues. We need to talk about these things. God created man and woman naked, so having sex, being fruitful, and pleasing your spouse is of God. What kind of person can come to church and please the people of the church but not the spouse in their own home? Are you more attracted to the church than you are to your own mate? Are you perverted in thinking that God would not want you to satisfy your spouse but wants you to come and please Him with your worship? God ordained marriage. When you choose to accept God, it does not mean that you dress up to come to church, but you turn your spouse off at home because you don't feel the need to get dressed up for them. You don't need to be old fashioned because you got saved. Women, your husband married his woman, not his grandma. Don't allow the enemy to come into your house because he will use power, money, or SEX to bring it down.

Don't try to use your children as an excuse. Youths age 12 and up are well aware of what sex is, and may know more than some parents, but we as believers must teach them from God's word what it is and how it is to be used. We must teach our children about why we abstain from having sex and what God says about sex, relationships, and marriage. Stop letting the television, Facebook, and the Internet teach your kids about these things. Many kids want to know about power, money, and sex, so they seek it out more than individuals who are preparing for marriage, and definitely more than those who are married. Children understand, and as adults, you should understand the desires of the other person, preferably before entering into the relationship. Many married couples have failed to understand these things in marriage, and their marriages have become routine.

The Love Level Connection #3: The *emotional connection*. This level is very important, so much so that if you are not connected on the emotional level, it will be very difficult to move forward in your relationship. The emotional connection deals with one's temperament, behavior, maturity, and confidence. This level deals with the state of mind or the emotions of an individual. For individuals who are extroverts or those who are highly charged, it would be difficult to deal with someone who is an introvert or who has a low level of motivation and optimism bordering on depression. If two individuals get together, and they are polar opposites as we have described, it probably will not work. One person cannot be insensitive and the other sensitive. You can't be the one that's trying to make your relationship work while the other could care less. Why? Because a relationship can't survive when two people are moving in opposite directions.

When discussing the emotional connection, consider this: Both women and men cry, but men don't cry for long. Women, if you cry, don't cry for long. Men are less emotional, and when you get hurt and keep getting hurt, they don't want to hear about it. When one person in the relationship keeps trying to get attention, a man becomes disinterested. This will eventually lead to arguments.

When God took woman out of man, she became the emotional side of man. This is why men are less emotional and they are no longer interested when a woman cries for too long. The woman was created and taken from man's emotional side. If you have an emotional disconnect, you lose the ability to communicate, and everything becomes sensitive to the woman. When everything becomes sensitive and you ask a man what's wrong, he will give you a brief response, because he knows that any conversation will just become an argument. Why do men respond to women, when asked what's wrong, by saying, "Nothing"? Men become private like this because they were built to be strong and territorial. They become defensive, and when they do this, women tend to think that something is wrong. Men are not as emotional as women because God calls men to guard the head and women to guard the heart. Although women may cry more, men get their hearts broken more easily. Women guard their hearts, but they don't guard their minds. Statistics indicate that more men commit suicide than women because of broken hearts or their inability to deal with broken hearts.

> I Corinthians 11:3ERV says, *But I want you to understand this: The head of every man is Christ. And the head of a woman is the man.[a] And the head of Christ is God.*

In the Greek language, the head means source. Man is woman's source, Christ is man's source, and woman is man's resource, and without this order they cannot renew. Woman is the one that reproduces or multiplies, but man is the source of the seed.

P.M.S. FACTOR (POWER, MONEY & SEX)

Most people have gotten married because they have kids and they, the kids, have kept many couples together. So what has happened? We got married and we did not plan for the second half of life; we only married for the first half of life. When you get married and don't plan for the second half of marriage and the second half of life, the game will end before the fourth quarter. What you were excited about in the beginning of your relationship won't excite you in the second half of your relationship. When you were young and youthful, things you did created excitement but now that you are older you have to create new interests and discover new things that excite the both of you. This is where you start to see desires lost because no new desires have been created. You are now settling for growing older together but not having a life. This is when the snake tries to come in.

The Love Level Connection #4: This level of connection deals with the *mental* capacity, and it is the most important of all the Love Level Connections. You have to know your mate's mindset. Can they handle rejection, acceptance, change, or judgment? Will they be able to deal with disappointment, trouble, or disagreement? This is extremely important to know, because when you marry, you are purposed by God to marry your soul mate.

Your soul mate is not just your lover, but also your best friend. Soul mates are whole, they are true lovers, and your soul mate is your alter ego. This side of you keeps you in check; you may even call them your evil twin, but only your soul-mate can deal with your alter ego, the worst side of you.

As lovers, you share your nakedness, but you can't tell your lover your worst secrets. When you find your soul mate, you create a godly soul-tie, but when the relationship is not of God, you create an ungodly soul-tie that will need to be broken. In a relationship with your soul mate, you invite someone into your life, and if you don't understand their mental capacity they may influence you and take control of your life.

In Genesis 3, Eve invited Satan into her relationship by speaking with him and establishing an ungodly soul-tie because of her desires, and because Adam failed in the 5 Ps. Eve struggled with her identity, trying to be more than what she was purposed to be. Romans 12:3, says, "Let no man think of himself more highly than he ought to think, but to think soberly." Eve had become self-seeking and had allowed the serpent to deceive her into believing she would be powerful with the knowledge gained from the tree. It was this perception and influence that caused her "to be drawn away by her own lust." James 1:14 , "But every man is tempted, when he is drawn away of his own lust, and enticed."

Eve lusted for power, and once lust is conceived, it brings forth sin and sin brings forth death. Her hunger for power destroyed her relationship with Adam. Eve's fatal attraction to the tree was a fatal distraction for Adam, one that he did not acknowledge or deal with.

Eve brought destruction to God's original plan for man and woman when she ate the fruit. How much influence does power have in your relationship? Either it's an issue and one person has all of it, or you have worked through some form of the love connections and you equally share the power in your relationship.

Do you know what the power factor is in your relationship? Are you unequally yoked, does one need more control, or is one of you lacking control, causing the other to be abusive? Have you entered into a relationship that created a co-dependency on the part of one or the other because of physical or verbal abuse? Has this power given one or the other the ability to manipulate or dominate the relationship?

When Eve's lust for power dominated her judgment, Adam blamed her, and she blamed Adam, but both were at fault.

So, let's wrap this up. At the beginning of this chapter we began discussing Genesis Chapter Three, and talked about Verse Six, where Eve was said to have liked the idea of gaining power. Then we began discussing the love connections, which are simple, yet meaningful, conversations every individual must and should take part in before getting into a relationship.

In James Chapter Four, we are told of how Satan crept into the garden. He was given an invitation by Eve. In Genesis Three, it does not appear that Eve is surprised to hear the serpent speaking. It also appears as though Eve is leading Adam, and the serpent was not even worried about what the man would do to him. Eve wanted control, and at some point she became less interested in Adam and more interested in what the serpent was saying.

Satan had made Adam and Eve move from "the spot", their place of worship, the place where they knew and worshipped God, and Adam had simply gone along with it. The Bible says that he was with Eve when she was talking with the serpent. In James Chapter Four, the Bible also tells us to submit ourselves unto God and to resist the devil, but a woman will not submit to a man that doesn't submit to God. Satan had calculated well because when God came to "the Spot", which was the place of worship and fellowship, man was not there. God looked for Adam, but Adam had hidden himself from God, because he said the woman told him that he was naked. So, who's blaming whom?

In tying this chapter together, it was necessary to remind you that this all began in the garden. It was in the garden that the deception began, because somewhere in the relationship, Adam became less interested in leading Eve and he began to follow her. We also see that Eve became less willing to submit when she begins to listen to the voice of another.

So what does this have to do with the love level connections? Everything. It reminds us that we need to be in a relationship that has been ordained by God, one in which we understand these four aspects of the relationship. When we build upon these connections, we build stronger relationships, and when we build stronger relationships, we build relationships that last throughout the second half of life and in spite of outside influences.

Chapter 3

Breaking Ungodly Soul-Ties

What is a soul-tie? A soul-tie is the knitting or attaching of two souls, and is related to the act of two souls becoming one. When a couple gets married, it is the acknowledgment of two people becoming one tying two souls together. When two souls become married or knitted together, it is because of a godly soul-tie or an ungodly soul-tie. Soul-ties are not created just between men and women, or between two people who are intimate. Soul-ties are created in friendships, parent-child relationships, even relationships between pastors and leadership.

Each of these relationships has the potential of being an ungodly soul-tie. Many people have them, and they think that things are working in their relationship, when in reality the only relationship that works is the one you have with God. A godly soul-tie can be referenced in relationships described in the Bible, such as Adam and Eve, David and Jonathan, or Ruth and Naomi. You will know that you are in a godly soul-tie, because when it's time to leave, you can't. It's a common mistake to think that you have found someone who can complete you, but in God we are whole, and we don't need someone to complete us. We need someone who complements us or makes us better.

When Adam saw Eve in Genesis 2:23a KJV, he immediately says, "This is now bone of my bones, and flesh of my flesh." In Verse 24 NASB, he says, "For this reason, shall a man leave his father and his mother and shall cleave unto his wife; and they shall be one flesh." For the joining of two souls, or the coming together as one, the vows of marriage were given and taken. This is a godly soul-tie, and for this reason, your emotions are now his or her emotions. Your heart hurts when his or her heart hurts and your pain becomes his or her pain. Your Partner understands that you don't want to be hurt, and he or she doesn't want you to be hurt. Therefore, you both take vows, swearing that you will be around until death do the two of you part.

Jonathan and David are an example of a godly soul-tie. Jonathan did not choose his father; he chose David over his father. When David began to depart from Saul, Jonathan realized that there was a covenant between him and David.

P.M.S. FACTOR (POWER, MONEY & SEX)

Ruth and Naomi's relationship also represented a godly soul-tie, an example of being unable to leave at a time when you feel you should, because the two of you are one. The relationship of Elijah and Elisha is another example of a godly soul-tie. Elisha was attracted to the God of Elijah, or to the mantle Elijah carried. When Elijah is taken up, Elisha catches the mantle, which was a part of Elijah. For Elisha, this also symbolized a double portion because now Elisha carried both mantles, his and Elijah's.

It's important to know who you're connecting with, because this person has to be as strong-spirited and strong-minded as you are. It's not good to be with someone and still feel alone, or that he or she doesn't understand who you are. What makes the two of you one is that you agree as one. The Bible says in Amos 3:3, "Can two walk together except they be agreed?"

Many people do not know whether or not they have their soul-mates, because they are still just hooking up with their lovers. A soul-mate is more than just a lover, or someone to get naked with. A soul-mate is someone who is a best friend and a lover. If you can tell your lover your secrets and the messed-up things you've done wrong without being kicked out and he sticks closer than a brother, then you've found your soul-mate. When you come into this relationship and establish a soul-tie, it will create a godly soul-tie.

In Proverbs 22:24-25, the Bible tells us to "make no friend of an angry man". Don't become emotionally bound, entangled, or wrapped up with someone who is controlling and influencing. In 2 Corinthians 6:14-18 KJV, the Bible says, "Be ye not unequally yoked together with unbelievers; for what fellowship hath righteousness with unrighteousness? And what communion hath light with darkness..." There are people who are caught in these types of relationships, and they are ungodly soul-ties from which they are unable to break free. Years later, they're still carrying baggage from someone else, even though they're trying to move on. Then, at some point, they finally decide to move on to another person or another relationship, but they're judging the new person as if they are still with the old person.

Many people have broken off old relationships – maybe even four or five relationships – but they still have the baggage from those relationships; they are still soul-tied to all of these individuals. So, the newly developed relationship was a fixation, or an attempt to move on and get over the last one – or the last four – relationships, but it's not working. Now you are in the relationship, and again you recognize or sense something from the past. Maybe this person wears a perfume or cologne that smells like Relationship Number Three, or maybe there are similar characteristics to Relationship Number One. Regardless of the similarities, you again realize that you still feel something for the former relationship, and have not let it go. Here again, you're in the new relationship, but you're comparing it to the old relationship, because you see the similarities from the old relationship. This is an indication that you are still soul-tied to one or more relationships. You may have said that you wanted a new relationship, or that you wanted to get away from the old, but there's an attraction to an old relationship that needs to be cut off. This is an ungodly soul-tie to someone in your past who was not your soul-mate.

There's a story in Genesis 34:1-3 of the Bible about Dinah, the daughter of Jacob. In short, Dinah went out looking for friends to hang with when Shechem, the son of Hamor the Hivite, prince of the country, saw her. Shechem took Dinah, laid with her, or had sexual relations with her, and he defiled her. Shechem raped Dinah, fell in love with her, and now was telling his father that he wanted to make her his wife.

This attraction is an ungodly soul-tie. Shechem was attracted to Dinah, forced himself upon her, and now he wanted her even more than when he first saw her. But this was not the custom of the people of God. In Verse Five, the story goes on to say that Jacob had heard what had happened to Dinah, but he did not say anything until his sons had come in from working in the field. Then Hamor, Shechem's father, came to commune with, or to have fellowship with, Jacob and to see about getting Dinah to become his son's wife. Jacob's sons became upset by the audacity of this man to ask for their sister's hand in marriage after what his son had done.

In Verse Eight, while Hamor is still visiting with Jacob and his family, he tells them that his son's soul longs for Dinah and how he, Shechem, would like to have her. But Hamor wants Jacob to give all of his women so they can all share in the wealth of the families and the land.

Jacob almost falls for it, but his sons say that this relationship cannot be so. They tell Hamor and Shechem that they cannot give their sister to one who had not been circumcised. Then, with a hidden agenda, they tell them that if every male were to be circumcised, that they will give them their daughters and the women of their families.

The reason for sharing this story is to bring to light the fact that ungodly soul-ties are created through attraction or attachment, and this attachment can begin in a good or a bad way. Nevertheless, this relationship is not a godly soul-tie, nor one with which God would be pleased.

When you allow ungodly soul-ties to continue, they pass on to the next generation, like sickness and disease. In Jeremiah 23, the people have been in bondage for so long that they begin to believe that they need to stay like that and not come out. Ungodly soul-ties create snares for generations to come, just as going outside of the custom and the will of God, creates wickedness that passes on for generations to come.

Signs that you are involved in ungodly soul-ties are loss of freedom; of the ability to think for yourself; and of control over your own thoughts, your own mind. The following situations indicate that you are involved with an ungodly soul-tie:

- Obsessive preoccupation with an individual to the extent that it causes you to neglect God, or preoccupation with someone with whom God has blessed you, instead of God
- Tendencies of being domineering and controlling in a relationship
- Symptoms of a Jezebel spirit, including deception, manipulation, or willingness to do whatever it takes to get what the person wants for himself or herself
- Difficulty with being truly forgiving
- Hearing sound bites or what seems like a recording of your relationship, or seeing fragments that look like a relationship from your past
- Experiencing a pattern of anger, blame, accusations, mood swings, or excessive crying over nothing

Ungodly soul-ties have patterns. These patterns trigger our anger, and usually the anger is over something trivial. You may also find yourself blaming everyone else for every problem or issue. If you find yourself crying about nothing when you're sitting there watching TV, or you go from laughing to crying, you may want to check yourself. If you see that you are attached to the scent of your ex's cologne or perfume, and start feeling emotions, or that you are hanging on to items from past relationships and they still cause you to become emotional, then ask yourself, "How much do they own me?" – because everything continues to remind you of that person you were with before, and what you may owe them.

In Genesis 29, we have another story of Jacob, in which Jacob is trying to find a wife. He has moved in with Laban, who has a spirit similar to that of Jacob. He too, is manipulative and cunning. Here, you should keep in mind that anytime someone is running from something, as Jacob was, they will bring that thing that they are trying to elude into the next relationship. The purpose in sharing this story is again an opportunity to show you how ungodly soul-ties are formed.

After seven years of working to make Rachel his wife, Jacob went into the tent and found Leah. He had been tricked by Laban, and agreed to work another seven years for Laban to obtain Rachel as his wife. In the course of the seven years, Leah is feeling rejected by Jacob, jealous of her sister, and hurt by her father, so she begins to have children. Although she was having children, she was not ready for a relationship, nor was she ready for marriage. She was only trying to live up to her father's expectations after being forced into a marriage. Leah is now learning about who Jacob is and the God that he serves, and she is naming her children because she is seeking the attention of her husband, who is lusting after her sister Rachel. After several children, Leah does not feel the love from Jacob that she wanted, and she finally understands and becomes attracted to the God of Jacob. She has her next son, whom she names Judah, which means praise. Leah's birthing of her sons represents a Love Level Connection she longs to understand and know, but it is not until Judah's birth that she took on the spiritual connection, and turns an ungodly soul-tie into a Godly one. Leah has become attracted to God, and has developed a relationship with God, also developing a soul-tie that was godly.

Chapter 4

Breaking Ungodly Soul-Ties (Part II)

When believers, or those in the body of Christ, refuse to talk about the issues of the world and to deal with those things that are facing and hurting people, we create some of the greatest ungodly soul-ties.

Men are attracted to women and women are attracted to men. They work together, play together and live together. They have friendships, companionships, partnerships, and all kinds of other relationships, but who is a soul-mate? And what is a soul mate, or what does it mean to be soul-tied? Who is the one that is God-designed for you? Who is your match, and why can't you find him or her? A soul-mate is your one true love. Your soul-mate is your alter ego, the other side of you. It's your evil twin, your companion, your best friend, or your kindred spirit. Your soul-mate is the one that complements you and makes you better.

Too many times we end up marrying our lover, but not our best friend. As lovers, you can share your intimacy and desires while you're being passionate with one another, but you can tell only your best friend your secrets, and you can only find a best friend through being a soul-mate or creating a soul-tie.

When you deal with soul-ties, it's not just about relationships between men and women. In regard to Jonathan and David, the Bible says in 1 Samuel that their souls were knitted together. Your best friend has to be your soul-mate, the one that you are going to spend your life with, because you're going to mess up, and your best friend will always be there. We have to be in the right place with someone with whom we are friends, someone we can talk with about our desires, wants, and needs. We want and need godly relationships, and some of these relationships will create godly soul-ties, and these soul-ties are healthy and okay for us to have. It is the ungodly soul-ties that create havoc in our lives and in our relationships. This applies to not only couples' relationships, but to every kind of relationship. It may surprise you to know that our greatest soul-ties have attached themselves to us as adults, and many of them since we have been in the church have come from those within the church.

P.M.S. FACTOR (POWER, MONEY & SEX)

When people come to the church, they are looking for someone they can trust, someone with whom they can share what is burdening them, just as the people in the church are looking to pour out what God has given them to share with certain people, but not everyone. So, we create soul-ties by opening ourselves up and allowing others to speak into us, over us, and for us. We give our trust to these individuals, because we believe that the people we are sharing our thoughts, issues, and concerns with are in support of us.

As believers in God, it is your responsibility to teach people how to find their destiny in God, not in you. We are to point them to God and to teach them about God. You are not supposed to lord over them with your thoughts about what God would do or say. You are not to speak as if you are a great authority on God and they should follow after you, but be supportive and point the way to God.

It's the dynamics of these situations that creates soul-ties. After someone who is in need of support or help confides in a believer, that person acts as if they are their responsibility and attempts to maintain influence over their life and their decisions; this ability to exert influence over someone's life creates a soul-tie. Once created, it maintains influence or control over someone's life or ability to make decisions.

It is Satan's objective to attack the things and people that God favors. He knows the favor on your life and he attacks this favor through soul-ties. He needs individuals, bodies, or people he can use to accomplish his plan, and aims to cause you to lose the favor of God over your life.

First Samuel Chapter One, Verses Four to Five in the NIV translation states that when the day came for Elkanah to sacrifice, he would give portions to Peninnah, his wife, and all of his sons, but to Hannah he gave a double portion. Hannah's name means favored by God, but it's ironic that God has closed the womb of the one He favors. It's interesting that the one wanting more is the one being given the most, but she cannot see it and does not understand why God has done what He has done. However, in the midst of it, she is still the one being blessed. It's because Satan will attack the one or the one thing that God favors. He knows the favor on her life, and he uses soul-ties to attack that favor. Hannah is soul-tied to Peninnah, and Peninnah was a willing vessel for Satan to use because she desired the attention or favor shown to Hannah by her husband. You have to remember that Satan uses

P.M.S. FACTOR (POWER, MONEY & SEX)

whomever and whatever he can, and he definitely uses soul-ties to get us off track.

Peninnah was a distraction to Hannah, and she caused her to get out of worship every year when it was time to go to worship. This was the one place that Hannah could connect with God and get clarity, and she would miss out, because Peninnah distracted her. Because Peninnah was such a big distraction, Hannah chose not to worship.

This situation is no different from a husband and wife getting ready for church, knowing that when they get there, God has something for them. However, something causes an argument, which leads to anger at one another. When they arrive at the church, they are so distracted that they can't get into worship. When you are soul-tied to someone or emotionally connected with someone to the point that you can't get into worship, you might want to check that relationship. If you know that someone is going to fight you over an issue, or if you know that someone is in competition with you, as Peninnah was with Hannah, don't compete. Don't argue with this person, and don't become distracted by this person.

P.M.S. FACTOR (POWER, MONEY & SEX)

In Luke Chapter 22 Verse 31a, the scripture states, "Simon, Simon, Satan has asked to sift all of you as wheat." Because the Lord had closed Hannah's womb, her rival (competition), the one who was obsessed with her, fights her the most.

Satan desired the favor that was on Hannah's life, that Hannah was not even aware she had. Satan lusts after people. He is obsessed with the favor on the lives of believers of God. Peninnah intentionally provoked Hannah, just to irritate her, and she was accomplishing what she had been assigned to do. Hannah's missing out on worship says to the reader that she gave in to it.

The difference between Peninnah and Hannah was that Peninnah had children and Satan knew that Hannah desired to have children. So the enemy can only use what you are supposed to have to keep you distracted. He uses someone to keep talking you out of what it is you are supposed to have or be doing. Whenever Hannah went to worship, Penninah was right there to distract her. Many of you make it to church, but you never make it into worship. Your conscience feels good that you made it to church, but your spirit never gets to worship because you are bound by your rival or your distraction. Hannah was so distraught over Peninnah, and her inability to give her husband a child, that her husband, in 1 Samuel 1:8, asked her why she was weeping, even after she had received a double portion, which in those times was illegal.

So ask yourself, why are you not getting what you need, when it's here for you to get? Haven't you received the Word of God for yourself after all of the times you've gone to the church, or have you not ever gotten to worship because you have been distracted? Have the people, as Elkanah did for Hannah, babied you, when they should have been helping you? In the church, many people have been babied when they should have been cut off. Because of the attachments, or soul-ties, that have occurred, they have not allowed individuals to be who they are in God. You did not hold them accountable for their actions. Accountability is about helping people be no less than you know they are and can be. It's not about making people feel good.

Hannah had the wealth, she sat at a table with plenty of food for her body, but her spirit was not being fed because she missed worship. Verse 10, of 1 Samuel Chapter One says that Hannah was in deep anguish, she was praying in bitterness and talking to God with irreverence. Then she made a vow, and she offered God a sacrifice. Her prayer changed, and she remembered that she was not a person of misery. She had let things get to her that should not have. She repented to God, even for her irreverent behavior and conversation to him as though He were a man. Something had attached itself to Hannah and had influenced her away from who she was. Hannah could not say to God what she really wanted, which was an indicator that the attachment had occurred.

When you find yourself entangled with someone, and you begin to act out of character, or you are unable to say to God what it is that you want or need, then you need to recognize the soul-tie, or the ungodly attitude, and give it back. Give back to them the attitude, the changes that were not you, and the behaviors that were not from you nor of God. Once Hannah got to this place in prayer, which was a place of freedom, she was able to continue on in prayer. When you get back in your place, others will come to you and invite themselves into your life to create another soul-tie; don't let it happen. Stop them from being nosy and guessing, because they aren't discerning anything. They are vultures sent to eat you up, not eagles ready to take you up. You've been here before, and at this place of vulnerability, you invited too many people in to hear your sad story. But not this time. This time, Hannah continued on in prayer and she did not care what the people thought. This was the place of worship, and a place where God could restore her and give her double favor. In 1 Samuel 1:15, Hannah's husband Elkanah had come to her and asked her if she was drunk. Be careful when you're in a place of vulnerability or place of restoration with God, because vulnerability attracts ungodly soul-ties.

If you become emotionally dependent on someone, or you begin a relationship in which you give another person power, influence, and your voice, you no longer have a say over your own life or over your decisions. Anyone who has this kind of control over you has created an ungodly soul-tie. Some may still feel free in spirit, but they are not free in their souls. Without a voice, you cannot make your own decisions. Anyone that can control your hurt, your rejection, or your brokenness has all of the power, and at any time they can push your buttons.

An ungodly soul-tie attached to your vulnerabilities can be one that attaches to the spirit of rejection, loneliness, insecurity, low self-esteem, fear, rebellion, or crisis. When an ungodly soul-tie attaches to rejection, it's attaching to the weakness of rejection; it wants to make you feel better. When someone who is accountable and has a godly soul-tie tells you "no", the ungodly soul-tie wants to comfort you in your wrong and make you believe that you were right, or that your thoughts or actions were right when they were wrong.

If an ungodly soul-tie has attached to you because of being lonely or a spirit of loneliness, it's attaching itself to that part of you that wants a companion, but is also willing to accept anything. The enemy will convince you that you are not lonely and that you are not looking for anybody, but that you just want a "friend". Many of you understand what is being said here and have found yourselves in this position. So let's stop right here and help you.

Being saved or being a believer in Christ did not stop you from being male or female. Sanctification should not change how you feel, nor should it stop you from being an individual. If someone has become attached to you in an ungodly manner, you will be unable to deal with your issues, because that person will control how you feel. Yes, it's okay to want a man or a woman in your life. It's okay to want a relationship, be married, and have a family. It's okay to be you, but be aware of these ungodly soul-ties to people who want to tell you how to feel and what you want.

Another attachment or ungodly soul-tie that is created by vulnerable souls is based on insecurities. An insecure person who becomes soul-tied to a person they see as offering a secure thing allows that person to begin controlling them through manipulation in the relationship, its finances, and other areas of the relationship. The insecure attachment may be to someone that always needs to ride with or to go somewhere with someone else. An ungodly soul-tie is created here that will allow that co-dependency to continue, instead of making that person accountable and responsible. This attachment is similar to an ungodly soul-tie created through low self-esteem or a low image of one's self. In this type of relationship, the enemy sends someone with whom you can be in relationship, and they continually tell you that everything is going to be all right. Even when you don't know how to handle trouble, this person tells you that everything is going to be all right because he or she has it under control.

Another type of ungodly soul-tie is one that is created from a vulnerability called fear. Fears or phobias may be the biggest ungodly soul-ties created. When someone can manipulate you based upon what you are afraid of, or when you think you're something that you are not, you can hear truth and reject it because you are afraid of the truth.

Many people can't establish healthy relationships because of some type of phobia. Many men suffer from genophobia, the fear of sexual relations or sexual intercourse. This is a man who will not give himself to a woman, because he feels as if he will lose his soul or other part of himself. But in actuality when two individuals have sexual relations, their souls become strengthened. The value of a relationship begins with sexual relations, because it is the establishment of a covenant, and each time that you enter in with each other, you are strengthening the bond between the two of you. When two people come into covenant they come into agreement, not into a relationship where one lords over the other.

There are also women who suffer from the fear of men, which is called androphobia. The same principles apply, but we find that women who have this irrational fear may suffer from this because of what they have seen in their lives. These women may have seen relationships where women were with men for years without ever getting married, and they don't want this to happen to them. But again, the point of sexual relations between married couples – as God intended – is to establish covenant, to come in agreement, and to strengthen the bond between the man and the woman.

In summarizing our discussion on soul-ties created through vulnerabilities, we will simply highlight the last two, which are soul-ties created through rebellion and crisis. The attachment to the vulnerability of rebellion is an attachment to someone who has been through so much hurt, and is looking for someone else to take away the hurt or to make them feel good about their state of mind. A rebellious attachment takes on the seven spiritual sins, and the seventh is an abomination to God. When people take on a rebellious spirit, they will soon fall. These people always want to be right. They argue about everything, and they never think that they are wrong.

The last ungodly soul-tie that attaches to a vulnerability attaches to the crisis or life-crisis vulnerability within an individual. These people can't handle turmoil, death, crisis, or being deeply wounded too frequently. In their vulnerability, they seek out someone who will be with them and let them know that everything is going to be okay. They may allow this person to linger in a depressive mode, or to linger in their feelings, and they do not hold them accountable.

How do we recognize these ungodly attachments or these ungodly soul-ties in our lives? How do we recognize the symptoms? If you truly want to be free, you have to break all ungodly soul-ties. Here are some things to look for:

1. You find yourself becoming preoccupied with someone else, or with his or her life; you find yourself comparing someone else's relationship to your own; or you are telling your mate that he or she should be more like another man or woman. You should know that what you are really saying is that you don't like who he or she is. This is a red flag.

2. You start feeling as though you are not getting all the attention that you desire. Jealousy starts when you get mad when someone is giving too much time to anyone or anything but you. Some people become jealous when they believe that you are giving too much attention to God. If this person starts making comments like, "You're doing too much for the church", but you have seen the changes that God is making in their life.

3. The other person becomes too dominating, controlling, or possessive. The person begins to have a takeover spirit, or wants you to be under or to look up to him or her. These same people will never have relationships with people who are confident about themselves. They will shy away from strong conversation and will prefer to hang with those that don't know much. People who are possessive or controlling gravitate to weak relationships, and when they feel like their companions are beginning to gain strength or confidence, they start to beat them down emotionally or even physically. They do not want others to feel like they don't need them anymore.

4. Be mindful of people who are manipulative; they try to control your time. They attempt to manipulate what you should be doing. They want to control you by keeping time on you. They create a fake need or grief to require you to give them more time. It's an ungodly soul-tie to control your time, just because they need it or want it.

5. Another symptom or sign of an ungodly soul-tie is mood swings, pressure, or uncontrollable crying. How do ungodly people form soul-ties with the godly? They open their souls to people who have what they want. Hannah had an ungodly soul-tie, formed by Peninnah,

the ungodly. How? Hannah opened her emotions and withdrew from Elkanah. What was occurring was a transference of soul-ties. Some of you have allowed people to come into your lives, and now you are living their lives, and they are living the life you wanted.

Let's look at the situation a little more closely. Peninnah's name means coral or pearls, precious jewel or gem, to turn, beautiful, or angel. Ezekiel 28: 1-14, calls Lucifer the beautiful angel, the precious stone, that turned ungodly, but taking from the term pearl, we must first understand how a pearl is formed. A pearl is formed through pressure and irritation. Before it's a pearl, it's a particle or piece of matter that has been covered in nacre, a defensive secretion created to protect the oyster from intruders. From multiple layers of secretion comes the pearl.

Peninnah was creating soul-ties through the emotions. She knew how to attack Hannah through provocation, through pressure. She endlessly tormented her, put pressure on her, or irritated her. Peninnah dictated transference to Hannah's soul. She caused Hannah to keep looking at her situation and to desire what had not yet been given to her. Peninnah had pressured her so much and so often until she no longer had to say anything or be around for the pressure and the tormenting to take place.

An ungodly soul-tie is one that takes you out of worship, even when that tormenting spirit is not around. Peninnah wanted Hannah's life, but in the biblical days, she was considered most blessed. Remember, the enemy is after our future and our favor. Your enemy will always see the better and greater things about you or your potential. Peninnah knew how to make Hannah look different in front of people or to get her out of character. The more Peninnah provoked, the more Hannah just came and sat in worship service, never being a part of worship. You will not be okay if you don't break the ungodly soul-ties.

Again, it's important to reiterate the necessity to not create ungodly soul-ties, and if you recognize that you have been in a relationship, or are currently in a relationship that is unhealthy or has the symptoms of an ungodly soul-tie, you can break the soul-tie. If you find yourself in a vulnerable state and are looking for someone to heal your vulnerability, don't do it. You break an ungodly soul-tie by recognizing your vulnerabilities, by knowing the symptoms of an ungodly soul-tie, and by getting back to a place of worship. You break the soul-tie through your spiritual Love Level Connection to God. You break an ungodly soul-tie by turning to God to meet your needs and not man or woman.

Chapter 5

Delivered & Blessed, but Still Broken

What does it mean to be delivered and still broken? Many have been delivered, saved, brought out of situations, and are even in church, but they are still broken. Many have power (authority), have relationships, and have kids, but they're still broken. Relationships cannot be successful when one person is broken or has no power. In a relationship, one cannot look for fulfillment and have expectancy of great things when the other is broken.

Broken is defined as the condition whereby your will is brought into full submission to His (God's) will, so that when He speaks you put up no argument or excuses, you just obey. There are two types of brokenness; one is to be broken by God, and the other is to be broken by man. To be broken by God is a good thing; to be broken by man is not. Brokenness is the experience of pain, suffering, or being forcibly separated into two or more pieces. Broken means to be fractured, in pieces or damaged. Broken relationships can be broken marriages, friendships, hearts, spirits, or souls. Broken

P.M.S. FACTOR (POWER, MONEY & SEX)

can also apply to people who are broken in their mind. Many people are on the cutting edge of change, but are mentally broken, and still there are some that are mentally well but physically broken. There are others who are spiritually broken, and it has caused them to become bitter, not better. Some pretend to be better, because life (man) has broken them, but they're still bitter.

In 2 Samuel 9:1-4 NLT, David asked if there was anyone left of Saul's house that he might show kindness to, for Jonathan's sake. David summoned Ziba, who had been one of Saul's servants, and Ziba told him that Jonathan had a son named Mephibosheth, and he was crippled. Crippled is another word for broken.

2 Samuel 4:4 NIV/NLT tells the story of how Jonathan's son Mephibosheth became crippled, and this story relates to the theme of being broken. Mephibosheth was not always crippled, but someone that he trusted, and who was entrusted to care for him, dropped him, just as someone has done to many of you, literally or figuratively. We can never put our trust in someone who can't handle it when things go bad, or someone that can't be trusted when things become shaky. We never put our trust in someone we can't depend on.

This inability to find people that we can trust has left many people broken as children and as adults. For those who were broken as children, the effects of being broken then still have an impact on you now. The reason for this may be because some brokenness can't heal on its own; some brokenness requires major surgery.

Mephibosheth was dropped at age five. As children develop, they become physically strong, mentally apt, intellectually prepared, and fundamentally able to learn. However, they need to be nurtured and cared for, all of their life, especially in the first five years, because these are the most important years of their lives. In this day and time, many people have become so busy that they leave their children with anyone, and they are often leaving their children in the hands of the wrong people.

Your child is a gift from God, and God has trusted you to care for them. When children are not cared for properly, they are left lacking mentally, socially, and physically. Because they have not been cared for properly, they are broken, and they pick up ungodly soul-ties. But because many adults are struggling themselves, they can't see that their children are struggling. The kids are struggling because their parents never deal with them.

Parents are too busy trying to work several jobs, and they leave their children with a young cousin, or a pervert, or someone that may be molesting them. Your children may be acting unseemly because you left them with someone you thought you could trust, but they fondled them; or you left them with an aunt or uncle who was suicidal and let them do crazy stuff. But if we are honest, many of you are this five-year-old. Many of you are adults, but you are still acting like kids, because you are still broken. You are still dealing with ungodly soul-ties.

These young children can't come to you, their parents, because they see how you, as a parent, are acting. You need help, yourself. Are you that person that was affected as a child, and because you are reading this book you now realize what has happened to you? Do you only feel good when things are going well? When things go bad, do you start smacking on the kids and cursing them out, but you're still speaking in tongues? Are the tongues that you're speaking curse words?

The problem is that your children are unstable because you are unstable. You are unstable financially, so they are unstable financially, and on and on. Ask yourself whether the relationship that caused you to put your family aside took place because you thought that person was heaven-sent, but now he or she acts like a monster. Does this person smack you around? Do you think that the broken person that you've become is who you are? Have you accepted that what you are going through is normal, when you used to have a dream and you had visions? Are you living now just to make it through the day because you are so overwhelmed that you think you're about to lose your mind? Then you need to know that this has to be broken, and that this is unacceptable to God for you. You are more than this situation and the circumstances surrounding it. You do not have to tolerate being broken any longer. Stop praying, "God just get me through this." Stop praying, "I want to commit suicide and I want to just get this life over." You can and will get through this, even though it may not feel like it right now.

Mephibosheth's name means to be an idol breaker, but he's broken in two. He himself now is just an idol and he draws attention to himself. But his name also means to exterminate shame. Being broken changes your assignment and what you are suppose to do. His name has two parts "Mephi" is a verb and "bosheth" is a noun. Mephibosheth was supposed to expose shame, but he lives in shame. When you're broken, the wrong people will start to manage you, and you will fall into the hands of someone you can't trust. You'll remain broken, but your condition is not who you are. You've just fallen into the hands of someone with his or her own selfish motives and desires, who doesn't know how to handle you. Mephibosheth, at the age of five, was preparing to be king, but being broken flips what he was assigned to become.

So now Mephibosheth is an adult, his feet are broken, and they send him to a place called Lodebar. Lodebar means to be in a place without passion. It means a place of desert, a place without covering or shelter, and a place of poverty.

When you're broken, you become attracted to the wrong people. These people don't want to manage you for who you are, they want to manage you for what you can be for them. So now you become a victim, because someone takes advantage of your vulnerability. This is why a man or woman who is coming out of a relationship rebounds quickly: He or she is attracted to people who smell vulnerability. This causes the vulnerable person to become intimate quickly, and to think that this is a covenant relationship, when the other people were never meant to be covenant partners. These relationships now cause the vulnerable person to become more dependent. The attraction is no longer based on incompetence, but wants.

People marry for a variety of wrong reasons. Many of you hook up because you're in church together, or because you say you're saved, but you're both just trying to be with someone who is safe. Many people have married out of lust rather than love. Some relationships that we keep trying to save are not meant to be saved. Some relationships were not brought together by God, and He may be bringing them apart.

Mephibosheth is broken at his feet. The word feet means foundation, and when your foundation is broken, you can't build a relationship. The problem is no one is trying to heal the brokenness and people won't admit that they are broken and that there is still brokenness inside of them.

So, Mephibosheth is crippled, but it has not stopped him from being in a relationship. He has a son named Micah, and this is just an indication that even broken people can still function and have children. In 2 Samuel 9-13, Mehpibosheth is approximately 21years old, with a child about the age of five, and he, like many others, now tries to live his life through his child and his brokenness.

Let's look at Jacob, another person who was broken. He has four wives and more than 12 children. He's running from his brother Esau, and he's broken.

How do you get away from brokenness? You break away from your past. God confronted Jacob in Genesis 32, and they wrestled until Jacob came into full submission. God wanted Jacob to choose a side. You have to choose who you will serve if you want to come out of the brokenness. While they were wrestling, God tells Jacob that he must let Him go, because the day is breaking. God is saying to Jacob that he can no longer hold on to Him while still holding on to what he has gone through for the last 20 years. Jacob refuses to let go, and God breaks his hip to bring him into submission. For 20 years Jacob has been blessed, yet he is still broken.

Anyone looking to break away from their brokenness has to break away from what they are still holding on to. This includes all of the pain, the old hurt, the

P.M.S. FACTOR (POWER, MONEY & SEX)

disappointments, the blame, and the shame. When you truly want to be free, and you tell God that you will not let go until He blesses you, God breaks you into something new, and you will no longer be able to hold on to what used to hurt you. You will not be able to cling to something that is no longer there. When God breaks you, it may hurt, but it will not cost you like it used to when man broke you. When Jacob lets go, he lets go of the past, and he takes on the new. He comes to the place where he knows who he is in God. Anyone who has ever been broken has to come to the place where they know who they are in God.

You need to tell yourself that you are becoming who you always were in God. You are a chain breaker, someone who can and has broken the cycle of brokenness. You can help others by talking with them where they are, and letting them know that submitting their lives to God will heal the brokenness they've had for their whole lives.

In relationships, we are physically, emotionally, spiritually, and mentally connected. This is why we are not happy, however; your soul deals with your psyche and your emotions. So if you try to use the spirit to fix your relationship, it will only quicken when it recognizes the spirit of God. It doesn't deal with the soul. You can't take the spirit home and expect it to change your relationship. It's not a spiritual thing, it's a soul thing. It's when soul-ties have been established that the relationship feels and is more permanent, but you can break the ungodly soul-ties. Psalms 19 says, the soul-ties that you should never have had.

When you are out from under covering, it makes you destitute. But if you are in a relationship with God, the Bible says in Psalms 23, "He maketh me (brings me into submission) to lie down in green pastures." How can you, as it says in Psalms 23, lie in green pastures, a place of rest and blessing? A place where God can still lead you, because the place where He lays you, not where you lay, is flowing with rivers of living water. This is a place where He restores your soul, a place where you manage your relationship again, rather than laboring in your relationship.

You have to understand that God is your shepherd; you cannot get into relationships wanting something that is not what God wants from the relationship for you. If you are in a relationship out of wants – and many people are – then more than likely you are being taken advantage of, either for your gift, your body, or something else, and the relationship will never work. If you allow God to lead you and to restore your soul, He will prepare a table before you in the presence of your enemies (Mephibosheth now sits at the King's table while Ziba serves him), and goodness and mercy will follow you all the days of your life.

CHAPTER 6

Can You Afford It?

Ecclesiastes 10:19 GWT: "A meal is made for laughter, and wine makes life pleasant, but money is the answer for everything."

The Message: Laughter and bread go together, and wine gives sparkle to life. But it's money that makes the world go around.

The purpose of this chapter is to talk about money. It's important when talking about money to ask yourself the hard questions. People assume that getting into a relationship because you like each other or have fallen in love with each other will make everything okay, but one of the top five reasons for divorce is finances (MONEY). So you need to ask yourself, can you afford it? Can your relationship afford what you and your partner are wanting, needing, and desiring? Did you count up the cost before you made some decisions or do now you wish you would have counted up the cost? If you're in business, or looking to start up a business, have you counted up the cost? Have you thought about the toll the business will have on you and your family? If you are in ministry, or are pastoring a church, did you not count up the cost? Or did you run out and get a loan that a membership of ten people can't cover? Before you decided to have children, with only one person working, did you count up the cost? Can you afford to do it?

If you are not in a relationship, this chapter will challenge you to think about these things before you get into a relationship. It will challenge you if you are single, married, looking to make some major purchases, or financial business moves, to count up the cost before you do it. Here are a series of questions that you should ask yourself, and truly reflect on, before you make your next financial move.

Ask yourself, "Can I afford it?" Because if you have not counted up the cost, it will not last. Can you afford the place that you live in? How much longer are you planning on staying there? Is this the place that you've settled with, or have you just accepted it? Can you afford the car that you're driving? How do you know that you can afford it? These are not questions of whether or not you have faith, or whether God will do it; do you have what it will cost you? Ask yourself why you are getting a new house. Maybe before you run out and buy another want, you should sit down and start planning. Write it out before you run out. Can you afford the new furniture or are you just getting it because you have always gotten new furniture every six months? What value does it have now? Can you afford to stay in that job? If so, how much longer? At what point do you start doing what you need to do and stop expecting God to keep giving you your wants?

Can you afford to eat out? If you have a big family and you're eating out three times a week, it's costing you about $50 each time. If you do that three times a week, you're spending $150. That $150 could go towards your electric bill.

Can you afford to keep being stressed out? Can you handle the backaches, frustrations, and sicknesses? Stress destroys your body, the temple of the Holy Ghost. When you're stressed out, it affects your relationships, and causes you to have ulcers and emotional issues. What is it costing you? Are you trying to keep up with the Joneses? Can you afford to stay in that job if you have visions and dreams? Can you afford to keep having a bad attitude and being unprofessional? Can you afford to walk in an employer's door with saggy pants, nose rings, and a loud voice? No, it will cost you that job.

Can you afford to stay angry? What is the cost of being angry? Anger can cost you your life. The first thing anger does to a believer is to take you out of fellowship.

Take a look at Cain in Genesis 4. Cain was worshipping in God's presence, but God stopped the worship because He sensed the spirit of anger. Anger brings on sin, and it's possible to be in worship and reject God all day and night because of your attitude or because you are angry. When Cain leaves the presence of God, he gives birth to sin. He exited God's covering and became revengeful, and in this state of anger and revenge, he leaves God's presence and goes and kills Abel.

Anger causes you to be out of control. It will cause you to oppose God and to kill what God loves. You think that God loves because of some reason, but God loves without reason. If you love with a reason then you've just killed that love.

P.M.S. FACTOR (POWER, MONEY & SEX)

Can you afford to be angry? Can you afford to stay unhealthy? Has the sickness left you or are you still praying that God will work it out? At one point, He worked it out, but not now when He has given you instructions on how to get better. You can't keep eating foods that you know will clog up your arteries or swim around your altar, which is your heart. Are you still smoking and saying to yourself that you bind the cigarettes in the name of Jesus? Are you saying to yourself while doing wrong that God knows your heart and you're expecting God to heal you?

Can you afford the relationship you are in? Can you afford the marriage you are in? Can you afford what you vowed you could afford? When you took your vows, you vowed in good and bad, in sickness and in health, for richer or poorer. Can you afford what you just vowed, that somebody else told you to say? What if the first time you heard it was the day you had to say it? Did you understand that you were swearing unto God? Understand that this is more important than all the vows. You have to understand that you are making this vow to the other person and to God. Can you afford it?

P.M.S. FACTOR (POWER, MONEY & SEX)

Can you afford to have certain friendships? Can you afford to be there when they need you? Can you afford being out of church, when you have true covenant? Can you afford to miss the Word that will bring you an eternal change, a season where God is getting us ready for Him? If you are not eternally changing here, you won't be ready for the Kingdom.

Can you afford to break covenant and be without covering? Can you afford to be disobedient, hard headed, or to shut out God? How can you, if you have so much God in you that you don't know where He's talking, where truth is being spoken? Can you afford to be disobedient? Again, ask yourself if you can afford these things, because God will always ask you to do what it is you say you can't afford, so He can show you who it is that co-signed for you to do as He wills. If it's God's will, it's God's bill. Review the scriptures in Ecclesiastes 10 and Luke 14 for more study.

Money issues are the greatest destroyers of relationships. No matter how great the relationship, when it starts having money issues, the relationship starts to have problems. I Timothy 6:10a KJV states, "For the love of money is the root of all evil." But Ecclesiastes says that money is the answer to all things, and in another translation, money makes the world go around, but the problem that many people face in relationships is that they try to have relationships in the name of love, but never get together just for love. If your love is not unconditional, then the minute they gain weight, spend too much money, or do something that you don't like, you'll fall out of love.

There are four types of love. Many people only know about "agape" love, which is the unconditional love that God shows us, but the first type of love is "phileo" love or brotherly love. The second type is "eros" a romantic or erotic love, which is probably the real reason most people hook up. The third type of love is "storge" a friendship or familial love. And the fourth type of love is "agape" an unconditional love, or a love without reason.

So what kind of relationship do you have? Ask yourself why you love the person with whom you are in a relationship? If you gave a reason, other than loving everything about them, you've just limited the relationship, because if you're loving someone for a reason, then what will you do when that reason is gone? Did you get with someone because they had a nice shape, or a pile of money? What will you do when that shape is gone or all the money is gone?

Love is not an emotion; love is a choice.

God chose to love us, and not because of how He felt. In the Bible, He says on numerous occasions that He chose Israel to love, He chose Abraham, and He chose Jesus, His son, to die on the cross. In John 3:16, God chose to love the world and He loved it so that He sent His Son to bring order to this world.

It wasn't until the New Testament that God gave the new commandment to love. How can you love someone and then place a condition on your love? In Luke 14, great multitudes followed Jesus, and He was not impressed that they wanted to be a part of His life. What impresses Jesus is when you know what, why, and whom you are following, and you bear fruit. If you are in a relationship and you are not ready to die for that relationship, then you're in the wrong relationship.

God so loved the world, but Jesus had to die. Love is designed to heal you and everybody connected to you. If you're in a relationship, you can't go on feelings,

P.M.S. FACTOR (POWER, MONEY & SEX)

because if you have a reason for your love, and the reason doesn't happen, you'll fall out of "agape" love and into one of the other types of love.

Everybody is looking for real love because love covers a multitude of sins. If someone says you can't have what you want, will you fall out of love? In Luke 14, Jesus told them if you want to follow me, you must first hate (epistio) your mother, father, sister, and brother. The word hate in the text of Luke 14 is Jesus telling those who follow Him that if you don't let go of what you have you can't be in relationship with Him. If you don't let go, every time that Jesus does something that you don't like, you will want to bring up your family to Him. Epistio means to refuse to hold to the past, to let it all go. If you choose not to let it all go, it will be difficult to be in covenant with Him. If you don't let it go and press forward, you will have to stay with the others. Even Abraham knew that he could not take his family when he took Isaac up to be sacrificed, because they would try to stop him. In 1 Kings 19:19-21 the KJV says,

> *So he departed thence, and found Elisha the son of Shaphat, who was plowing with twelve yoke of oxen before him, and he with the twelfth: and*

Elijah passed by him, and cast his mantle upon him.

[20]And he left the oxen, and ran after Elijah, and said, Let me, I pray thee, kiss my father and my mother, and then I will follow thee. And he said unto him, Go back again: for what have I done to thee?

[21]And he returned back from him, and took a yoke of oxen, and slew them, and boiled their flesh with the instruments of the oxen, and gave unto the people, and they did eat. Then he arose, and went after Elijah, and ministered unto him.

Have you truly asked yourself if you can afford it? Have you counted up the cost? The Bible teaches us that no man can build a tower without having first counted up the cost. You can't start something and not finish. In other words, you can't be in a relationship with Jesus if you can't afford to continue to build or if you cannot finish. How we love Jesus will determine how we love others.

Two of the most disqualified men in the Bible talk about relationships – Solomon , who has 300 wives and 700 concubines, and Paul. They both have much to say about relationships. In Ephesians 5:25, Paul talks to us about love and the relationship between men and women. Paul, who has never been married, has much to say about the subject. Paul, whose gift is that of celibacy, teaches some of the most important things about relationships, and he can say these things because he has been anointed by God to say them.

When you talk about love, you need to understand what God intended, what God says is love for a man and love for a woman. In Ephesians 5:25, God tells husbands to love their wives. In Ephesians 5:22, God tells wives to submit yourselves unto your husbands, but He does not tell the woman to love her husband. Why? Because a man does not need love, but a woman needs a man to give her love. In Ephesians 5:33 it says, "Nevertheless, let every one of you in particular so love his wife even as himself; and the wife see that she reverence (respect) her husband."

A man does not need love; he needs respect. If you try to give him love he'll walk away, he's not turned on by love, but if you give him respect, he'll stay. A wife is turned on by someone giving her love, but this is why relationships are destroyed. We are not doing what we are supposed to do for one another. A man's strength is his eyes, and a woman's strength is her hearing. She needs to hear that she is loved, and man only needs to see. When a woman gives her husband respect, which means praise, he will love her more and be willing to do more. A man does not know how to go back and build the foundation, so he needs to be praised to stay built up. A woman needs to stay loved so she can stay covered. The Bible tells wives to submit, but it tells husbands to love their wives as Christ loved the church.

To the man, his wife can do nothing to cause him to stop loving her, because to love her as Christ loved the church is not eros love or storge love; it is agape love, unconditional love. Christ loved the church so much that He died for it. He had to die for the sinful church, so if Christ died to cover the world's sin, then you should know that if you die for your wife, that you will get back up.

When a wife takes a vow, she submits to her husband. In Ephesians 5:33, the Bible tells the man to "so love his wife even as himself." Why would man love woman like he loves himself? Man should love woman as he loves himself because woman came out of man and because whomever you're with should be a part of you. If the other person ever hurts, you should already know that he or she is hurting without being told. In Ephesians 5:33b, the Bible says that the wife should "see" that she respects (reverences) her husband. A woman's strength, her hearing, also became woman's weakness, because Eve listened to a serpent that got her out of her place. Why did she submit to the serpent? Because she had lost her husband's vision.

Think back on the discussion of Leah. Leah did not get Jacob's attention until she birthed her fourth son, Judah, whose name means praise. With this son, Jacob fell in love with her. If you learn how to praise your man, you will get the love, attention, and affection you're seeking. After the birth of the first three sons, Leah was seeking the other types of love, but this time Jacob would love her because she praised His God and him. Jacob could not love her until she praised him. After Judah was born, Jacob stopped giving as much attention to Rachel, and he turned to Leah.

In Genesis 2:25, Adam says that this is bone of my bone and flesh of my flesh. A woman is birthed out of a man's womb, or his pain, and this is why she needs to be loved. For her, affection is love. Many times it appears that man is insensitive, but he isn't. If you praise him, he'll show you love.

Verse 24a in Genesis chapter 2 KJV: "Therefore shall a man leave his father and his mother." This is not for one person to lord over the other, but from the foundation, God knew that two people could not be one unless they left the baggage, and all of the other stuff, behind. This is not to say you cannot go and visit your family or talk to your family. This is so that the two in a relationship would be one.

In Luke 14, Jesus is telling them that you have to give up the parental authority, he did not marry your parents and you did not marry his, but if you break covenant, you lose your rights. If one is beating the other, then you have broken the covenant, or agreement, between you and the parents.

So now this couple has to cleave, and to cleave means to chase, and this is not happening in relationships anymore. When a woman no longer cleaves, she has lost her aggressiveness, she stops running. The Apostle Paul says that he is running after something that he is trying to cling to, and as long as he is in pursuit, he will long to cleave. Wives, don't lose your aggressiveness, give him something to chase. Women, it's praise that arouses the man; and men, it's you telling a woman that you love her that will turn her on. Can you afford this relationship? Can you afford love?

Chapter 7

Throw it Back

You will always catch what is attracted to you, and you will always know what (or who) is attracted to you by the bait you use. So what have you been catching? If you don't like a certain type of man or woman, then you need to change the bait you are using.

What's bait? Your conversation is bait. You will catch people who are attracted to how you talk. If you talk hustle, then you will catch hustlers. Or are you cunning, and have been caught by a cunning fish, just to find out later that it's an eel fish. Are you shocked to find that you haven't caught what you thought you had? You caught an eel, and they give off electric pulses that shock people. Why did you catch this snake or eel? You didn't know what kind of bait that you were throwing out there. Eels like to hang out in dirty water, but when they've had enough, they head off to fresh water to be cleaned. Are you tired of being shocked by relationships? Are you ready to get to some fresh water?

Have you been in a relationship so long that it has become dirty, polluted, stagnant, and shallow; and you've become dirty, as well.

So, you've realized that this is not what you want, but that you want more? The Japanese koi fish has the potential to grow to over 4.5 feet in length, but it has to be placed in the right environment to reach its capacity. In a fish tank, it will only grow a few inches. In a pond, a little larger, and in a lake, a little larger. But in an ocean, it can reach five feet. This same fish always had the potential of reaching 4.5 feet but it was always dependent upon its environment. Who or what is in your environment, and are they keeping you from growing? Many people want more, but continue to hang out in the same circles, or environments, with others who don't choose to grow.

If you can't leave the circles you're a part of because someone is mad, or because others are not growing, you may want to look at those relationships. In Luke 5, which is parallel to St. John 21:3-6, Jesus wanted to teach the Disciples, and he starts by teaching them about patience. In contrast to the Disciples, today's generation has a microwave mentality. They do not want anything that they have to wait for. For them, it can't be good when something cooks 40 minutes in the oven when they can get it done in three minutes in the microwave. Jesus is trying to teach the Disciples a lesson. He's teaching them that they have not caught anything, but they have to be patient, because they are there to help someone else. He wants them to be patient while doing ministry, to be patient when helping others, and to know that He understands how it feels to have a need, but you're serving others who have the same need. Are you questioning God; how can you do for someone else when you, yourself need the things that you are doing for someone else? Jesus teaches the Disciples patience, temperance, and how to wait for God. While they are being taught, people's lives are being changed. God will never give you what's yours until you help someone else.

God is trying to teach you to work with something or someone, one on one, until you can work with what He gives you without losing it. The problem is that you keep trying to get to promise by yourself. Whatever you were anointed to do in the previous season, you can't do the same thing in this season. When you know who you are, the deep calls unto the deep. In this season, you will connect with someone who will hook up with you and be able to pull out of you what has been inside of you all the time. No one has to sprinkle any magic dust, or anything else, on you. You just have to be in agreement with someone who knows how to pull it out of you. God will never give you what's yours until you stop looking for something magical or easy, just because you don't have patience. How can you be a fishermen without any patience? Stop being a procrastinator and an instigator. You're losing focus too easily, because you're trying to hustle your promise, but if it's your promise, why do you have to be sneaky and crafty?

In Luke 5 Verse Four, God tells Simon to launch out into the deep and let down his nets. They catch so many fish that they signal for their partners, and their nets begin to break. In John 21, Jesus is at the beach cooking fish, but he's asking the Disciples if they are still struggling to do what they know how to do? Jesus wants to teach them how to get provisions. He tells them to go down and throw their hooks in the water; the first fish that they catch will have provision.

People have to learn how to wait for what is theirs. If you are going to fish, you must have patience. In this season, you will not just use anything for bait because you are not just expecting anything. In order to catch more, you have to reach out into deeper places, and in this season, you won't catch something average because you won't be fishing for something average.

He tells them this time to use hooks, because this time they will need bait. Peter threw his out from the place that he was in; he threw out into the deep water, because it's not about this season but the season to come.

People are not catching anything because they keep using the same bait, but not in the right season. Many of you keep ending up with a snake, and you want God to keep giving to you, but God says you've got to get up and get it yourself. A good fisherman will not settle for just anything, and if it's too small, he will throw it back. You keep catching catfish, bass, or brim, but this time don't eat the fish, throw it back. Never eat what has given you provision.

This season we are not fishing for bass, koi fish, or brim, but blue marlins, and you can only catch blue marlins in the deep ocean. On average a small marlin is four to five feet long. Ask yourself if you are trying catch that size. If you have decided what you are going after, have you changed your bait? If you don't change your bait, you will still catch the same kind of fish. You will not be able to catch something bigger if you are trying to use the same bait that you used in a pond. You can't be shallow and think that you will catch a marlin. A blue marlin doesn't want worms or little fish, it's attracted to tuna and shrimp, and to get something bigger it's going to cost you more.

If you're trying to catch a marlin, you won't catch it on the shore, or in a little boat. You have to understand what you are trying to catch. The marlin has expensive tastes, and wants tuna and shrimp. Do the people you're hanging with still want worms on the hook, or do they want shrimp?

Watch people who will try to talk you out of going to the deep place, because they settle for the mediocre. Tell your friends or whomever you hang with that if they don't want more, they can move on. You'll be able to tell who these people are by the bait that they go after. Look for those who still want your old bait, those who are not attracted to the more expensive things, and get rid of whatever is attracting them to the bait you now have.

A blue marlin has an intellectual capacity and doesn't go straight for the bait. He has patience, and understands that he doesn't have to take the bait. In this season, you are about to catch more than average, and this catch will be bigger than you. Don't try to just pull in what you've been waiting all your life for. In this season, you will have to give and take, you will have to do whatever it takes to bring in your blue marlin, the one that you are supposed to have in this season, because it's worth it. In this, you have to trust and know that what God promised you is bigger than you, and if you don't trust you'll go back to thinking that the bass is more than what it really is. Stop chasing something that you can't do anything with. In this season, throw some things back, don't just pull it in because you can. In this season, don't ask God for more when you're still in the shallow place. Ask yourself if you can afford to not go out into the deep.

Some of you think that your man or woman is trying to hurt you, but they really aren't; they are trying to get your attention, but they're going about it the wrong way. In this season, quit trying to be in a relationship with a male or female who doesn't understand that you need to change before God fixes the relationship.

Chapter 8
Help, I'm in Lust

James 1: 13-15 The Message:

> *Don't let anyone under pressure to give in to evil*
> *say, "God is trying to trip me up." God is*
> *impervious to evil, and puts evil in no one's way.*
> *The temptation to give in to evil comes from us*
> *and only us. We have no one to blame but the*
> *leering, seducing flare-up of our own lust. Lust*
> *gets pregnant, and has a baby: sin! Sin grows up*
> *to adulthood, and becomes a real killer.*

How many of you are in lust? To lust simply means to
have an appetite for something, to be hungry, to be
lured, to be infatuated or fixated, and to fantasize. To
lust means to be drawn away from your environment,
or to take on your own voice, because you have lost
your way, and it still appears that God is speaking to
you. To lust means to create your own dreams
because of your own fantasies. You begin to create
your own stipulations and rules outside of Him. Lust
means to be enticed. Love gives, lust takes, it has its

own agenda. But love has an agenda for someone else. You lust for someone or something not intended for you. When the enemy sends a lust spirit, it will always call you away from God, but God will always call you to Himself. You'll recognize lust when your eyes are opened up later, and the same thing you lusted for drives you crazy.

Lust gets you and your life out of control, and it cannot be controlled. There's a difference when you don't know who to love and this is uncontrollable, but lust makes you out of control, and makes you do things that you would normally never have done. It makes you become someone else. It robs you of your identity. It teaches you to believe that you are somebody else.

Lust is why you struggle with the house, the car, the man, the woman, or the job, because maybe it was not intended for you, but for someone else. Be careful when you say that you are so in love with someone and you can't live without them, because maybe when you can live without them, you'll discover that it wasn't love but lust.

Agape love never changes. Have you ever prayed and asked God for something, and shortly after He gave it to you, you couldn't stand what it was that he gave you? Either the payments on the car you wanted, or the job you wanted? Be careful what you pray for, because it's not just you and God in the conversation. When you pray, you are litigating either on your own behalf, or on someone else's. Anytime there is a litigation going on, there is a prosecutor looking to stop the petition or the favor, because now the enemy knows what you want or desire. Satan is without strength and power when we are in God's presence, but what happens when we are weary and about to faint? Satan senses our vulnerability. Don't be foolish enough to think that the enemy is not hearing your prayers. Be careful that you are not judging others with your own lustful sin, because when temptation comes, you will fall harder, because you don't believe that you have any temptation (pride), but the sinner will just fall from sin.

When Satan hears our desires, he turns them into lust and tries to lure us away from God's presence before God responds to our request. What happens is when we appeal to God we become weakened and vulnerable, and Satan tries to use this temptation to lure flesh out. The Bible says let no man think he is standing when he has fallen. No one has room to judge another individual.

People are tempted by Satan in one of three ways.

1. The lust of the flesh

2. The lust of the eye

3. The pride of life

He did this very thing to Eve in Genesis Chapter Three. Eve is lured out because of her own lust, vulnerability, and desire for power. He tempted Eve with her lust for power. The enemy has to lure you out, because you cannot have this conversation in the presence of God. So he creates an illusion, or causes you to be intoxicated, or to appear to be drunk. The enemy does not want you going forward; he wants you to go backwards. He wants you to get out of God's presence, to walk out of God's light. For most people, it is hard to think when intoxicated. Satan lured Eve out of God's presence, from the Tree of Life, by the lust of the flesh, and then the fruit. When he lured Eve out, she was at the Tree of Life, but now she is at the Tree of Knowledge. He tempted her with the lust of the flesh; when she saw the fruit, she said that it was good. Then he tempted her with the lust of the eye;

she saw that it was pleasant to the eye. And then he tempted her with the pride of life; she knew that it would make her feel more powerful. Eve was becoming someone else, someone that she was not intended to be, through her own lust and vulnerability.

Many people lust for someone else's life. In Exodus 20:17, the Message translation, says, "No lusting (coveting) after your neighbor's house – or wife or servant or maid or ox or donkey. Don't set your heart on anything that is your neighbor's."

If you're wanting or coveting something of your neighbor's, then you are lusting. If you want someone else's life because you don't like something about your own life, you're in lust. Many things you lust for but cannot digest, because it was not intended for your body. When you wish to have someone else's marriage, and you are coveting their relationship, you are in their life or their bedroom.

Eve is lured because she wants more, and this is the same for the body of Christ worldwide. The leaders in the pulpit are promising them more, by telling them that they are great, and that they will be wealthy, when in reality many of them cannot handle $100.

P.M.S. FACTOR (POWER, MONEY & SEX)

You can't tell people that they will be more without taking them through the process. When you are out of the presence of God, who's speaking to you? Satan. Now that you are out of the presence, you can't hear God. Satan lured Eve cut, and her desire for power was the bait, but she was the bait for the man. Satan wanted Adam, and Eve left him uncovered.

Eve wanted to be crowned. She wanted all the glory for herself. She was tired of praising man. Never hook up with anyone who wants it all, because lust does not share; lust is simply, pride. Eve is now out of the presence of God and has taken on the lust of the flesh. If you take on the lust of the flesh, you haven't got out of the Spirit, but her own lust will make her believe that she is still in the presence. Once she takes on the lust of the flesh, she now has an appetite, so she eats the fruit. Her eyes are wide open, and she gives it to her husband.

Adam, who had followed the bait, is now outside the presence of God. He takes of the fruit, he swallows the pride of life. God, up until this point, had not moved. He did not move until Adam ate of the fruit. God can handle someone not wanting the crown, but He couldn't handle that no one managed what was His. When your house is out of order, make sure you're still doing right by God. Somebody needs to avoid becoming intoxicated, someone has to stay saved in the house, and in the relationship. When Adam ate of the fruit, death took place.

There are four types of deaths that occur when you get out of the presence of God: spiritual, social, financial, and natural. This is what will happen when one becomes vulnerable and lust comes in.

The first death is Spiritual, and we know that God told them that immediately when they ate of the fruit they would surely die. We know that Adam did not die naturally, but He lost eternal life.

The second death was social or relational. It killed the relationship; people no longer see God in you.

The third death is financial. When you get out of the presence of God your resources get cut off. All of the resources Adam needed were in the presence of God, where the four rivers flowed. Deuteronomy 8:2 says that the blessings of God will overtake you. You have become magnetic, and people will give to you because they are attracted to success. In His presence, there is fullness of joy, you don't have to try and manipulate people in His presence.

P.M.S. FACTOR (POWER, MONEY & SEX)

The fourth death was a natural death. He (Adam) died in Genesis chapter five after he birthed Seth, who was birthed in his image and likeness. Because of their sin, they birthed pain for women in child-bearing.

Temptation, covetousness, weakness, and vulnerabilities all lead to lust, and it's giving in to our desires that draws us out of the presence of God. The greatest temptation sometimes comes through who you love. If your house is out of God's presence, you will not know His will and you will not hear His voice. You won't know how to love without being in the presence of God, because outside of God's presence there is no love. Don't let lust get you out of character or cause you to lust after other things or other people's lives.

In Judges 14, Sampson goes to Timnah, sees a woman, and tells his father to give him the woman. Why? Because he has been tempted by the lust of the eye. His father tries to talk him out of it, but the Lord found an occasion to use Sampson's decision, even with his bad choices, to get glory in the end.

God will turn your lust into love. Today is the day that you come back to God. Tell God that you've allowed your lust to get you out of His presence, but your love

P.M.S. FACTOR (POWER, MONEY & SEX)

has brought you back. You have come to the conclusion that you will lose everything, but you cannot afford to lose God.

Chapter 9

Toxic Relationships:

A Dysfunctional Man and a Dysfunctional Woman.

2 Samuel 4:4 ERV:

> *Saul's son Jonathan had a son named Mephibosheth. He was five years old when the news came from Jezreel that Saul and Jonathan had been killed. The woman who cared for Mephibosheth picked him up and ran away. But while running away, she dropped the boy, and he became crippled in both feet.*

There are some things, some people, and some relationships that you are carrying, though they have the ability to walk and run on their own. You're carrying them, and you shouldn't be. This does not mean that you don't love them or don't want them, but you are hurting the one that you are in a relationship with. For example, in 1 Chronicles 4:9-10, the Bible says, "Now Jabez was more honorable than his brothers and his mother called his name Jabez, saying, 'Because I bore him in pain.'" Jabez's mother was hurting and, because of her pain, like Rachel, she named her son Jabez. Both of them neither cared nor understood what they were doing to their children. Jabez's name means to cause pain and sorrow, and from the day he was born he was rejected. As a child, and even into adulthood, he caused others pain. Although he and his mother were in a developing relationship while he was in the womb, and because that relationship caused her pain, he would know pain for a large portion of his life. She never gave him a chance, and Jabez had to break this power and influence over his life. He chose not to live in bondage. He learned of his lineage and he called on the God of his family to take away what he saw in the mirror of punishment. He did a self-examination, and overcame the strongholds of self-feelings, and God honored his request.

Another example is Mephibosheth. Mephibosheth's mother is not mentioned, but the story begins with Mephibosheth's caretaker, the one who loved him, dropping him. She loved him too much. She didn't trust Mephibosheth's ability to walk on his own. Never try to carry foundation. Foundation is naturally heavy. Biblically, the feet represent a foundation, and many people are trying to build a structure without a foundation. Mephibosheth, now crippled in his feet, still has stimulation or the ability to be stimulated. Ensure that you are not so focused on trying to help people's extremities that they become dependent on you. Don't be the one who is helping someone who's crippled when they still have stimulation.

Mephibosheth couldn't get a job or take care of himself, but he could make babies. How is it that this crippled man has a son? Who carried him and laid him down somewhere to have sex? If someone has the ability to do that, then they have the ability to get a job. The problem is that there are too many Mephibosheths in relationships with their care takers. Some of you have married Mephibosheths, some live with or are in relationships with a Mephibosheth, some of you are raising Mephibosheths, or paying for their mistakes, but they still have stimulation.

Mephibosheths have the nerve to talk about having favor when someone is doing everything for them. Mephibosheths have desires, but they have no passion. If you're in a relationship with a Mephibosheth, you may be in a toxic relationship.

Toxic means hurtful, harmful, poisonous, dangerous, or deadly. At some point, toxic relationships, no matter how much you love someone, will die, either quickly or slowly. Whether it happens quickly or slowly, a toxic relationship, is still a toxic relationship, and it will die. Such relationships are accompanied by psychological, emotional, and mental abuse and will eventually result in psychological trauma.

Toxins destroy everything that makes you, you. They create anxiety attacks because they become too overwhelming. They create chronic depression, which always brings chronic disorder; they create post traumatic disorder; and you begin to lose yourself. You are becoming someone else, and the stress on your mind is causing you to have a nervous breakdown. In a toxic relationship, you become unstable, and you can be laughing one minute and crying in the next.

Toxic relationships happen in the Bible. These relationships are how the enemy attacks strong people, people such as Elijah and Jonathan. **Here are some signs to help you identify whether you are in a toxic relationship:**

1. In a toxic relationship, you can do nothing right. There are very few compliments. In fact, there are more criticisms than compliments. You are criticized for how you open the door, the way

you talk, the way you sleep, you can't cook right, and you don't smell right. You're always being put down. In the body of Christ, many people lose their confidence because, while they can fight the negativity of the world, they can't fight it when it comes from those who are supposed to love them.

2. Everything is about the other person, and nothing is about you. He or she will out-talk you or talk over you to prove a point.

3. You cannot make your own decisions, because someone is controlling you or taking over. If you're in a toxic relationship, it will rob you of your confidence and make you feel like what you used to be good at, you're no longer good at.

4. You lose your identity; you become someone else's property. In a toxic relationship, you begin to be abused by someone who is misusing the scriptures for his or her own benefit. If you're in an abusive relationship, and you've lost your mind, and now your partner wants to take your body by using the scripture that says 'your body belongs to him or her'. This person is perverted

and wants to pervert you, due to an inability to understand scripture. He or she no longer consecrates the relationship, but rapes the other in the relationship. This relationship has become so toxic that you no longer know who you are and you are willing to follow anything or anyone that sounds like scripture. You just go along with what anyone says because you are no longer in a relationship with God. Every time you are with this person, he or she is releasing more poison. This results in loss of balance, vision, and purpose. Why? Because you have opened yourself to a person who has dropped you, someone who didn't know that you could walk on your own.

5. In a toxic relationship, you are not allowed to grow and change. You'll know this because the other person in the relationship wants to keep you as you have always been. Too many of you are being smothered in relationships. It's not romantic; it's sick. Something that is being smothered isn't getting nourishment, sunlight, or rain. In a toxic relationship, the controller intimidates you and what you won't do willingly, they force you to do through threats. Anytime

P.M.S. FACTOR (POWER, MONEY & SEX)

someone needs that much leverage or control, he or she will always be intimidated and afraid to lead. People who are this afraid of losing other people always end up by themselves.

From Genesis to Revelation, participants in toxic relationships are tortured. The aggressor looks for reasons to argue and torture. If this individual loses the upper hand, he or she will look for ways to gain that control back. When the aggressor in a toxic relationship has used every other tactic, you lose your options. If you are no longer willing to do what you've been told to do, the way the other person tells you to do it, when he or she wants it done, you will be forced to do it.

Too many people are being tortured at home. Then they bring that spirit into the church and expect someone to sing them out of it. In a toxic relationship, one individual is being tormented at home, on the job, and at the church, but they are choosing not to be free. This is no longer just what is being done to them; a spirit of vexation is now controlling them.

In the Bible, Saul has this spirit of vexation, and now Mephibosheth has it as well. The only thing that he's got going for him is his father, who had a relationship with David. Saul never dealt with the spirit. He was always ministered to by David, but he never dealt with the spirit. Many of you have this spirit, and it makes you dysfunctional, because you are always wanting someone to minister to you. You have to be in a relationship that is genuine, authentic, and ride or die loyal. Stop getting into relationships that are stimulating, sexual or fixed up, because if someone has to pick you up, they will eventually drop you. Mephibosheth always wanted to be ministered to, this was something that came down from his grandfather Saul. This is the problem, this is where the dysfunction began.

Your problem is predicated on those who have ministered to you, but when people don't compliment you, your whole day becomes messed up. The reason some of you are threatened by another is because you don't feel that you can totally satisfy your mate, so you talk down to others. Saul did, but he never confronted the spirit of vexation. Never become so hurt that you can't tell somebody you've hurt that you're sorry. The power is never in someone forgiving you, but in you forgiving them.

In toxic relationships, you want to control the outcome. You want to control what's coming in and what's going out. But what happens is double jeopardy. You want people to keep being killed over something that hurt you. Saul died bitter. He was king, but David had already replaced him, because God never leaves someone in place that can't forgive someone that is out of place. This is why Jesus came and took our place; we were out of place.

Chapter 10

What a Woman Wants and What a Man Needs

Do you know that it is impossible to love without being loved first?

Do you want a balanced life? If so, you'll have to keep God's original plan in mind while reading this chapter. You will need to understand why God planted a garden and left man naked. If you are naked, you should never be ashamed when you are with the one you are supposed to be with. You only have to feel ashamed when you are not with the one you are supposed to be with. Job tells us, naked we came in the world and naked we will leave, but in the church, people don't want to talk about nakedness. Some say you shouldn't say this or that in the church, but if they read their Bible they would see where God talks about nakedness and sexuality many times.

What the church wants to do is put clothes on everything and everyone. They are too religious to realize that there are a lot of fake-it-to-make-it hypocrites in the church, and all they want to do is to cover up their nakedness and that of others. In Genesis 38:6-11; 13-21; 24-30 HCSB, you can learn why mistakes continue to be made in relationships. When you refuse to grow, to learn, or to improve your condition, God kills the issue or the person. In Genesis, Judah's son Er was evil, and God killed him. His brother, Onan, was told to go into Er's wife, but Onan released his seed, his sperm, on the ground, and God killed him. There is life in your seed, and when you waste the seed on the ground, it says that you don't want to consummate the relationship you are in. In the seed is life, and when you waste it, you won't produce as God intended.

So Judah tells Tamar, his daughter-in-law, to wait until his younger son is of age. The scripture goes on to say that Judah had lost his wife and he was getting ready to go sheer sheep in Timnah. When Tamar learned that her father-in-law Judah would be coming through town she changed from her clothes to a harlot's clothes. Many of you are familiar with harlots outside of the church, but what about those on the inside, the temple harlots. She changed her clothes, veiled her face, covered herself, and sat in the way of Timnah because she knew that Shechem had grown up and she had not been given to him.

Make sure that you are not in a relationship with someone who has covered his or her face. Don't let the tongue talking in church mess you up, because the same one that speaks in tongues can curse you out.

Judah saw Tamar and thought she was a harlot. He asked her to come and sleep with him. She asked Judah what she would get for sleeping with him. Judah offered her a young goat, but she said no, she requested his signet ring, staff, and cord, and on that day she was impregnated. In Verse 19, she gets up, puts her widow's clothes back on, and is not to be found for several months. Judah is later confronted with the information that Tamar had been acting as a harlot, and is now pregnant. Now, Judah hears the information, and judges Tamar for what she has done, but he is in denial of what he has done.

Watch people who will judge you when their sins have not been brought to the forefront. Tamar identified the man who had gotten her pregnant, and Judah had to concede that she was more honorable than he was.

Let's identify with what Tamar, a woman, wants and what Judah, a man, needs. Most women want you to

P.M.S. FACTOR (POWER, MONEY & SEX)

"put a ring on it", but is it a sex trap? This may seem far from what is taught in church, but church is where this should be taught. These next few pages are not about what's not happening in the church, but about God's original plan for a man and a woman becoming one. Being married does not make you one. It's only through consummation that a man and a woman become one. God's plan was that man would share the same relationship with his wife that man shared with God. He wanted man and woman to know that love is sacred, but that it is also a place of worship when you are with the one with whom you are supposed to be.

Before there was a tabernacle, God created man and woman to be a tabernacle. I Corinthians 6 says, "Do you not know that your bodies are the temple of the Holy Ghost?" Men and women go through a certain process before getting married, and the mistake we have made is not going through this process, which gets you into the place of worship. The first thing that should happen is in Proverbs, where the Bible refers to "a man that finds a wife," not a woman looking for a man. He is to present the woman to God for approval.

The problem these days is that you find someone or something, then you name it and claim it, but you don't want to prove anything. The first thing that

P.M.S. FACTOR (POWER, MONEY & SEX)

happens when you get to the tabernacle is that you have to present your gift to the priest. Then the priest will take the gift and examine it. However, the problem that many people face is that we examine the gift, but we don't give it to the priest or to God to examine. This examination period is what we now call premarital counseling. According to God's standards, the relationship would not go any further if the priest does not accept the gift. In the Bible, there is no such thing as dating or courting. When you find the one you believe is to be a part of your future, you would start counseling right then. This is important, so that you don't waste months and years just to find out that he or she wasn't the one. Then the priest has to examine the gift, and some gifts don't take a whole lot of examining because at the first altar you'll know whether or not they are the one. Once the priest examines the gift and says it passes his inspection, he now puts it up before God, so that the Father can bless the relationship.

Once you have come out of counseling and the priest, pastor, or preacher says that you can go onto God, he also indicates some things that you may want to consider as you go. If there is anything that you need to keep hidden or unsaid, you need to put a stop to this before it goes to God. If you or the priest recognizes that there are some flaws with the gift, you need to reconsider before presenting that gift to the Father.

If you recognize something that your spiritual father, pastor, or priest would not be pleased with, then why would you want to present it to God? Why would you want to be in a relationship with someone who is not consecrated or in covenant with God? Hooking up with someone that is not hooked up with God is messed up. Whoever you are about to marry should know that you are holy and that there is nothing going down but what you want to go down. You are to present your body as a living sacrifice that is holy and acceptable. This is your reasonable service.

So, women, when you decide to marry, you give up your legal rights to your body, which means that as you are consecrated and worship God with your body, your body is consecrated and holy for your husband. For your husband, your body will be a temple that is sacred and holy, which is your reasonable service. This means, women, that you give up your rights to your body and you give up your name. Women, when you decide to get with someone, don't get with someone whose name does not mean anything. When you are willing to sacrifice your name and your body, you're giving up a lot. This is why counseling with the priest was necessary, because as a woman you are giving up a lot, and have not gotten married yet. This is why the goods were not to be tampered with before marriage.

Once you've presented to the priest, God has to approve the relationship, and for God to approve the relationship, the priest and the people all knew that the smoke had to go up and vanish. If the smoke came back down, God did not approve.

Once the relationship has been inspected, tested, and approved, then you move to the court of praise. If you are in covenant with God, then you should never hook up with someone who does not know how to praise. This is why the picture of the tabernacle is like a marriage. People are made up of three dimensions, but typically we only operate in one, the body. But what about the soul and the spirit? Relationships have difficulties because people deal with them in one dimension, the body.

At the tabernacle, once you go through the outer court, you reach the brazen altar. At the brazen laver, you are washed, and here is where you should be sure that this person is the one. Again, you have another opportunity for inspection. The brazen laver is the place of purification that comes after inspection and testing. You need to be clear before you go through the cleansing. Is this person the one you are supposed to be with? This is also where it's hard to break ungodly soul-ties, people with whom you have entered into relationships. Now you know that none of these people was the one.

At the brazen laver is where there is cleansing, purging, and a washing away of sins. Before going any further, you have to forgive anything and everything that may have hurt you, or you will experience the old baggage. Here is where you have to be healed before you can go to the next place of consecration; where you destroy, cut-off, and cast off every ungodly soul-tie; where you take your relationship out of the public and consecrate it with your partner. The opinions of others no longer matter. After you've been cleansed, no one on the outside can speak into or contaminate your relationship. This is why the tabernacle is a picture of marriage. In order to have the marriage that God intended, you have to go through the process.

The next place in the tabernacle is the Holy Place, and in the Holy Place you have the shewbread, the lamp stand, and the incense. You need all three of these things in your relationship.

The shewbread represents the breaking of bread, fellowship, and communion. Before any lovemaking goes on, there has to be friendship. The shewbread represents communion; you take communion in a relationship, when you take part with one another's bodies. You are in communion and friendship, but relationships mess up when all they are is lovers, with no friendship. You are exchanging one another's body when you take communion. After making love, lovers don't have anything to talk about and now their relationship becomes contaminated. This is because someone in the relationship needs to talk, and does not have anyone to talk with, so they go back outside the relationship. So before anything else, we take communion, we find out what kind of friends we have, because only real friends can commune with you, learn all of your dirt and still be your friend.

Next is the lamp-stand, which is to illuminate or enlighten. You have to be in a relationship in which you can be enlightened, so that in a time of darkness the other person can reach the dark place within you. You need to be hooked-up with someone who can see when one of you gets out of the will or out of the presence of God, and has gone to a dark place. You need someone who can minister to you. The lamp never blazes, but it trims; this is to say that you don't have to jump all in, you need to be with someone with whom you can be intimate without the touching. If you feel that the only way to be intimate is to do something, then you don't have someone with whom you can be intimate.

The third thing you need is the incense. The altar of incense smells of sweetness. You always have to have an air of sweetness in your house. Never let disagreements cause you to be unpleasant or disgruntled. So when the enemy comes, he won't think that he can live in your house with you.

Now, comes the part of the process in which you need to go beyond the veil. Many of the priests could not go beyond the veil. You had to be more than just a priest; only the high priest could go beyond the veil. In your relationship, the man has to know that he is the high priest, that he is the only one that can go beyond the veil. Going beyond the veil is the final stage of marriage. This is where the high priest takes off all of his clothes, or the man takes off his and the wife takes off all her clothes and the two are naked.

P.M.S. FACTOR (POWER, MONEY & SEX)

Beyond the veil is the mercy seat, but in order for the atonement to work, there must be the shedding of blood. Everyone knows that when a virgin has sex for the first time, she bleeds on the organ of the man. For the atonement to work, blood has to be shed on the organ of the man. The organ of the man, or the testicles represent the man's altar. God gave man two testicles to be a witness to his seed and the consummation. After ejaculation, the testicles are a witness to his seed. This is why when a man climaxes into a woman, it cannot be denied that this is his seed; the testicles give witness. This is also why man was not to waste his seed. The seed produces life, and if you waste it, you kill the power of the blood. Without the shedding of blood, there is no remission of sin, and it's the remission of sin that makes two become one. There has to be blood for the two to become one.

If you study the tabernacle, notice that there is an altar before you go in the gate that was designed for God. There is also an altar before you go into the Holy Place that was designed for relationships and beyond the veil was a place designed for the high priest. Here you are now covered in blood, just as God has covered you in blood, and nothing but the blood can wash away sins.

P.M.S. FACTOR (POWER, MONEY & SEX)

If you disagree with what is being said here then go and study Genesis 17. The Bible tells us that as God speaks to Abraham, He tells him that He made him a promise, but it will not come to pass until we cut covenant, and this time we are not cutting covenant in the spirit and in the soul, but in the flesh. To God, covenant is the cutting of flesh; God circumcises man as his mark of covenant, and even Jesus was circumcised. The cutting away was done on the eighth day, which symbolizes a day of new beginnings. The old has been cut away.

Beyond the veil is another area where relationships can go bad, because when man releases his seed or sperm, it's not just semen, he releases his soul into the woman. So when the woman goes to get up she didn't just know him, but she laid with him.

Some women have a whole lot of souls within them, and this is why it is hard to break the ungodly soul-ties. Many people think that when they are with a man or a woman, a sexual relationship is all it is. However, Leviticus 17 tells us that the life of the blood is in the flesh (nefesh), or the soul. It may help you to remember that the soul is tied to our emotions, and this may be the reason that many who are in relationships walk around with so many mood swings.

They have so many ungodly soul-ties with so many others within them.

The life of the seed is so important, because it produces soul-ties, whether they're godly or un-godly. This is what the enemy is after. He wants you to keep producing ungodly soul-ties. The problem is that when you keep having sexual relationships, you keep producing ungodly soul-ties, but, again in Leviticus 17, it says that when you produce seed you produce soul. So looking back at Tamar, she has recognized that she has been used by Judah, and it causes a good woman to become bitter. Many women are bitter because they have been hooked up with the wrong men. Tamar is patient, she waits for Onan, but Onan did not understand that his seed had purpose. Judah tried to deceive Tamar, and go on with his life while she was waiting on the youngest son to come of age. Be careful with people who have not received what they think they are entitled to, because they become bitter and bitter people set up "sex traps". They start to feel that they have waited long enough, and when they see that it looks as though they are not being considered, they start to think of sex traps.

So Tamar takes off her widow's clothing, portrays herself to be a harlot, and puts on a veil. She knows that every man's curiosity is to know what's on the other side of the veil. But just as Tamar is thinking about traps, so are many others, because so many men have had bad relationships and they messed them up. But what about the good men who created godly soul-ties?

So who is Tamar and why did God stop everything to tell us about her? Tamar's name means abundance, it also means to date, not as we think, but in reference to time. Her name also means palm tree, upright, to be erected, or to cause arousal. Because of Tamar's ability to stimulate men, many of them couldn't handle her. Perhaps this is why the others died, but when she gets with Judah, he doesn't die. Judah is more mature, and Judah is praise, so anytime you get praise and a palm tree together, you'll have a harvest. Her name means not to settle, so when Judah tries to give her a goat or a kid, she knows her value and does not settle. Tamar does not settle for the goat when she knows he's a sheep keeper. He was trying to cheapen her, but she tells him that she wants the signet ring, his cord, and his staff.

Tamar wants the signet ring because she knows her value. She wants others to know that she has a man, and that he has glory. The ring means commitment from the man. The ring symbolizes oneness and covenant. The ring means everlasting, eternal, always increasing in value over time. It may look like it's worn out, but it still has God, and when it's cleaned up, it will look like God. The ring also represents identity.

The second thing that he gave up was his bracelet. The bracelet represented everything he owned in those days. Because Judah was vulnerable, he gave up everything he owned when he gave Tamar the bracelet. The bracelet was like a Black Card; it had no limit.

The third thing he gave up was his staff, which signifies power. So now Tamar has his name, all of his valuable possessions, and his power. What does he have left? All that Judah has left is praise. All that he has of value is praise. So for you, when you have lost everything due to a relationship, you've still got praise, and praise will get you back to where you need to be.

So what does a man need? A woman needed three things, but a man needs four things, and together that's seven things: perfection. Sometimes you have to give up what you want to get what you need. How do we determine what a man needs?

P.M.S. FACTOR (POWER, MONEY & SEX)

In Luke 15, the Bible tells of a man who has fallen. To get back up, some of you men just need to come back home and first be recovered or covered. The first thing the Father gives him is a robe. When he puts the robe on, it represents royalty, and takes him from rags to riches.

The second thing he gives him is a ring. A woman needs a ring for commitment, but a man needs a ring to show support. A man doesn't show his ring off but it lets other men know that he has a good thing. For a man, it signifies that he and his wife have merged all of their valuables and that they collectively are more than they are separately. It signifies that he has a good home, and that they are one.

The third thing that he gives him is shoes. In a relationship, it's important for a man to have shoes. The shoes signify that he is in a relationship, but not in bondage, to the woman. To be without shoes is to say that the man is in bondage. To have shoes says that the man is free, he can breathe, but he does not want to be smothered. He needs shoes because he's got work to do. No strong man wants to be barefoot. He wants to put on his traveling shoes without a woman thinking that he's not interested in her, or without a woman thinking that he doesn't love her. He wants the woman to know that we've got places to go. A man who is smothered is passive and soft; you don't want a woman to have to speak for you when you're a man and can talk for yourself.

The woman cleaves, or clings, to the man, but the man chases. When a man stops chasing, or cleaving, it takes the excitement out of the relationship, and now the relationship has no room to grow. The relationship now becomes routine, and neither wants to tell the other that they want to be out of the relationship.

The fourth thing the man receives is a celebration. Any man who has been beaten down or abused needs a woman to celebrate him. Women, men need your praise, because women can endure more than men.

So we have Tamar, who did not get pregnant by Onan or by Er, but by Judah. When Judah finds out that she is pregnant, he leaves. During childbirth, the midwife ties a scarlet string on the hand of the child who should have come out first. But, unexpectedly, the child that should have come out second is born first. His name was Pharez, a child of breakthrough. In this season, those who have struggled in relationships, marriages, or friendships are going to come out running. You won't land on your head. This is a time of breakthrough for your relationship and for you as individuals. Judah gave you praise, but Pharez gave you the ability to break out or break through. Now is the time to enter back into a place of worship so you can get an unexpected deliverance.

Chapter 11

Breaking the Cycle

(John 4:4 - 10; 16-18 NKJV)

In John Chapter Four and Verse Four, Jesus had just left Judea, and He tells the disciples that He needs to go through Samaria. At the well of Jacob, Jesus speaks to a woman, and He asks her for a drink. She says to Him, "How is it that you, being a Jew, ask a drink from me, a Samaritan woman?"

As you continue to read, more of the story will be highlighted, but the purpose is not to dwell on what you have heard concerning this story or what it is you think you know. This story has many parallels, and they will be identified as you continue to read. What is important for you to get out of this is how to break cycles.

Jesus has to break a cycle; He has to destroy a myth that has become a way of life. He has to destroy what has come from someone's superstition, mythology, religious beliefs, or some other type of belief system. The problem is that many people are believing in something that they think is truth, but it isn't the truth. When you've heard something for so long, many people assume that it's truth. The concern now is that you're passing on an untruth to other generations, and you're still living a lie. Those to whom you pass these beliefs are living a lie, it breeds into their sociological beliefs, and their social relationships become messed up. You're at the point where you are confronted with the truth, you try to spiritualize what you need to deal with in the natural, and you need to deal with the things you've naturalized in the spirit. All of this has created an imbalance for you, and you're not sure what you need to do.

So we need to break this cycle. The cycle keeps happening to you, not allowing you to move forward. The reason that this keeps being a cycle for you is that you understand that every time God gets ready to bring you out, or to do something for you, you fall into the same habits and make the same decisions, because the problem looks the same. But it isn't the same. The enemy uses the same ploy, plot, or snare to get you caught up, and you fall for it again. A cycle is repetitious, it is repeating the same sequence, but in your mind you think that you are doing something new. In a cycle, you can't do something new, because you keep doing something old. You may be living in a new time, in a new year, but it doesn't make it a new season. You're still living in a day, but you're not living in the moment. We, like our ancestors, have fallen for the same errors and mistakes. We are taking new blood and covering it with old blood, but none of the blood has remission.

Someone has to own up to the mistakes and the errors made by our ancestors. Someone will have to say that if we want to get out of this, we have got to stop making the errors and the mistakes of the past. Deciding to change the way you think to become better is no disrespect to your family history or who they were, but if following traditions have kept you in poverty, maybe it's time to break the cycle. You have got to break the cycles so that you and the generations to come can get where you are supposed to be. If you want to break the cycle, quit blaming everyone else for how you are living. A cycle caused the children of Israel to be in the wilderness for 40 years, but, even worse than that, they were in a cycle of bondage for 400 years. Somebody has got to break the cycle.

The children of Israel go through a 40-year cycle, because every time that they are about to come out they fall for the same mistake. Every time God was ready to take them over the Jordan, they began to complain. You will always know when God is about to bring you or your generations out, because the grumbling and complaining gets louder. The reason that you hear the complaints and grumbling more is because it's a trick of the enemy to cause confusion. When God is about to do the miraculous, as He promised you, instead of praising, you complain.

Stop complaining and start praising God; don't wait until you are sick in your body or until you need something to praise God. Praise God before the trouble begins. God inhabits the praise of His people. He lives in it, and takes up residence in your praise. When you become more optimistic and more positive, you become more energetic. When you become more energetic, all of your thinking becomes positive. When you become a positive thinker, your heart flutters with joy, and out of the mouth the heart speaks.

The enemy knows that when you get close to your assignment, or your destiny, that only you can cancel what you're supposed to have. The children of Israel continue to fail in this 40-year cycle of what is supposed to be promised for them, because they refuse to be obedient and to quit being rebellious. The only thing that cancels out promise is disobedience. To

P.M.S. FACTOR (POWER, MONEY & SEX)

disobey God is to rebel, and there is no excuse for rebelling. The reason that people rebel is because they get more focused on the blessing than the one blessing. Don't allow what God does for you to change you, for you. What God does for us is to change us for Him, not for us. So, in every 40-year cycle, they get to the place of getting ready to go into promise, and they start complaining.

So how does complaining take place, or how does it start? Through conversation. Before any relationship can take place, before touching, kissing, or sex, it starts with a conversation. The greatest level of intimacy comes through conversation. If you are at a place of complaining, then you have drifted out of the presence. You cannot be in the presence of God while complaining. To God, complaining is a turn-off. When the Children of Israel would complain, it's as if God hits mute in heaven, because God only wants and inhabits praise.

Intimacy always begins with conversation, which means to commune. Communication is to commune, when you take part of one another. To commune is when one is broken, you know how to make them whole again. This is the start of a conversation. A relationship is designed by God to keep bringing out a

138

greater glory. If your relationship is about a bunch of stories, but it's not bringing out any glory, then you need to check your relationship. The Children of Israel circle the wilderness for 40 years, and Moses finally catches the mistake. You can't break the cycle unless you catch the mistake. Moses comes to the place where he realizes that what they were doing was a cycle. He says that they can no longer circle this mountain. Have you ever gotten to the place where you realized that there was a cycle happening and it needed to be broken? Did you realize that something had to change? That something had to be different? That something has to stop and it has to stop now? Tell that cycle: "NEVER AGAIN." This cycle has just been broken.

How did the Children of Israel break the cycle? There had to be a changing of the guard. In order to get to the next place, or to get where you are supposed to be, you have to change guards. Moses recognized that he could no longer lead the people to promise, because for 40 years he allowed them to complain about where they were going. Relationships cannot go any further when no one changes guard and declares that they can no longer talk about where they have been, but they must talk about where they are going.

Joshua now takes the lead; he did not change foundation, but began to implement a new structure. You cannot be in a new relationship without the cutting away of flesh. So the first structure Joshua implements is that there has to be a cutting away of the flesh or a cutting of covenant. For 40 years, they had been in the wilderness, and no one had been circumcised.

The second thing that Joshua says is that no one will do anything until all are healed, get up from here and cross over, because you cannot move forward until you are healed. You don't begin a new journey and get healed, you are healed before you begin the new journey. You cannot come in covenant with the old and the new. This is why God's original plan was for man and woman to both be virgins until the day they were married. On that day they would cut blood to consummate the relationship. They would never experience old relationships, old soul-ties, old boyfriends, and old girlfriends, while being connected to something new. This is the problem with those trying to go into new relationships; you still have old soul-ties, old problems, old bitterness, and old relationships connected to you.

P.M.S. FACTOR (POWER, MONEY & SEX)

The greatest intimacy in a relationship is when you don't have to say anything, and you're in agreement. It's when the other person doesn't have to tell you that he or she is hurting, because you know it, or when you just know that the other needs to be comforted. Because of the intimacy, it's the icing on the cake when they touch you at the right time, in the right place. When you're intimate, it's their look or their stare that gets you aroused. When the Israelites get to Jericho, the greatest level of communication is to say nothing. Even the law says you have the right to be silent. The best thing to say when you don't have anything to say is nothing, study to be quiet. So after six days of being quiet, when they finally talk, walls come down, because they're no longer complaining but thanking God because He brought them through it.

At the well of Samaria, Jesus has *five levels of communication*. Here He approaches ministry differently from any other time. Why? To show diversity and versatility. In relationships, you can't try to get people to change when you are not subject to change, you can't always want people to come up or come down; sometimes you have to meet them on middle ground. You can't just reach people the way you want to reach them. Jesus met the woman at the well on middle ground. He met her at a neutral place of Jewish ground and Samaritan ground. He came to the place where if He crosses over the well, He breaks covenant with the ones He's in fellowship with. The problem here is the well, the thing that she calls worship. The thing that sometimes destroys relationships is how we worship. The real problem is that the two of you don't have an agreement on how to worship God.

The first level of communication is the social level, or social communication. It is how every relationship should begin. The problem in many relationships is that they do more than just have a social level of communication. At this level, there should just be dialogue, or conversation, and it does not go any further than that. At this level of communication, dialogue is all you need to know. For one to find a friend, he must first show himself friendly.

If you go further than social communication, then you have moved over levels. The way you will know if the person is the right person is by their mannerisms and ability to communicate on the same level. If you don't have anything in common, then you'll know that you don't need to take the conversation any further. If you are a sophisticated person, you don't want anyone stepping up to you and saying something in just any kind of way. The way that someone approaches you will tell you whether or not you can have a conversation with them.

The social level of communication tells you that you won't run out of words. That if we don't go any further than this we can still be friends. When you are at the same social level, it tells me verbally that if we don't know anything else about each other, our dialogue says that we can be friends.

Never show, tell, or reveal to anyone your wounds, unless they have scars and if they have hurt, please don't share, because two hurt people don't have anything in common but their hurt. The two of you will be attracted to one another because of hurt, and you will build a relationship based upon hurt. You will never have healing in common, because all you have in common is hurt. Many times in relationships, we are attracted to our likes, but later you discover that you have the same hurt. Two hurt people can't heal one another, because they have the same hurt. At this level, you don't need to touch anything, embrace anything, hold anything, kiss anything, or feel anything.

The second level of communication is spiritual. Once you have determined that you can have a conversation, the next thing the person needs to know is how you love and worship God. At this level, the two of you need to know if you share the same beliefs, if you have the same course of destiny. Oftentimes, men come to church to find wives, but they still go to the club to find women. They want the good wife, but they also want the freak, but where women mess up is that they have already been asking God for a man for a while, and they have asked for a sign, so when the first man shows up and says you're supposed to be his wife, you jump at it. But what the man has seen or fallen for is the spiritual side, and when they get home he expects what he saw in you during worship, and that's not what he gets. During this level of communication, if you can't communicate spiritually, you will spend the majority of time arguing about church, because that's where the other person is happy. You need to know their level of spiritual maturity, because someone just going to church doesn't bring balance.

There is a spiritual level of communication where you are talking and you share the same core, both of you believe in the kingdom, in miracles, signs, and wonders. At the same time, you can love them as an individual, and still be able to speak in tongues. You don't want to be in a relationship with someone that gets bored with God, because if they get bored with God, they will get bored with you. Jesus tells the woman, at a social level, to give him a drink. Watch people with whom you can win when you want to give them something, but back up when you ask them for something.

The well of Jacob was where they showed up for fellowship and worship, but you have to understand the time when the woman showed up. Women did not come to the well at noon. All of the women showed up in the morning, so this is an indication that she was ostracized by the other women.

The third level of communication is the mental level where you talk about ideas, facts, and concepts. This is where you deal with things of the mind. Do you share the same concepts or a similar mindset? Do you share the same intellectual capacity? Here you can't be fake because you have to talk about things, or be able to explain yourself, what it is you think and why. Never invite anyone into your life who can't handle that you have changed, because they will discriminate against everything you do. At this level, you need to know the debt that you're coming into, any extra-marital kids, and how you will handle them, and who gets what. So, Jesus does not humiliate the woman, but his job is to get her to see the truth.

The fourth level of communication is the emotional level. It's the hardest, because it deals with the soul and the emotions. It is the most sensitive part of a human being. It's where all of the hurt and debris is. A broken soul causes a contrite spirit and a confused mind. The emotion talks about the wants, the needs, the aspirations, and the fears. It talks about vulnerabilities, and you can't be in a relationship with someone who can't handle your transparency. The other person must be able to handle that you are good and bad, that you have flaws and make mistakes. The mind and the soul make you get real personal, and you will try to get out of uncomfortable positions.

The fifth level of communication is when you can communicate for the one that you are in communication with. When you become socially, mentally, spiritually, and emotionally in conversation, and nobody has to say anything. The one with whom you are in a relationship can perceive and understand what you are going through, and you can cover them,

P.M.S. FACTOR (POWER, MONEY & SEX)

and cause them to deviate from where they are going when they get off track.

There are three types of communication. The first is proactive communication, where you communicate before something happens or comes. The second is reactive communication, where you respond to something bad, with negative words, or negative communication. Reactive communication is when you communicate out of reflex, anger, or hurt, and you can't take it back. The third type of communication is radioactive communication. This is poisonous, deadly, or hurtful communication. This is when you are out to kill. You are beyond hurtful words; you want the words to kill.

When Jesus deals with the woman at the well, she knew what to say socially and spiritually, but when it came to the mental category, she said that this is what we were told. Jesus asked her where her husband was, and she said that she had none. Jesus said that she answered correctly. He told her that she had been married five times, and she hadn't gotten it right yet, and even the one you are with is not the right one. She keeps showing up at the well every day looking for something out of the same cycle. She went to the well every day, but she didn't draw or drink water. She

147

went, knowing when men showed at the well, because she was looking for security.

He then tells her that when He first started talking to her, and He had impressed her, she thought that He was the one. She had built her relationships off of spiritual impulse. Why did she spiritualize her relationships? The well was where Jacob found his wife, Moses found his wife at the well. Intimacy and covenant always start at the well.

When Jesus tells her that He could give her living water, she was ready to jump into another relationship with someone she didn't know, because she wanted security. Jesus tells her that they could not have a true conversation until she spoke the truth. Never build a relationship on the highs of who you are, because when the other person sees the lows, he or she won't be able to handle it. Don't build a relationship on the greats, when all you got is McDonald's money. You'll know when you are in a real friendship or relationship when you don't agree, but you don't become disagreeable, and you are able to still hold hands.

P.M.S. FACTOR (POWER, MONEY & SEX)

Author's Communication:

This book could have gone on for many more chapters, and at some point it may continue, because of all that the Lord wants to say concerning relationships. We have touched on three major areas of relationships, but as you can see these three areas comprise much about relationships. There truly is much more to add, but we pray that you are blessed by the words of this book, and by the Spirit of God that has given utterance, and the anointing to say the things that were said and to teach the things that were taught. God's word has so much to offer concerning relationships, and we pray that this book will cause you to study and to learn more about what He has to say.

We also would like to thank you for choosing this book to read. We know that you had many choices when you found this book, but we know that it was God's divine Spirit that led you to choose this book on relationships. So we thank you and pray that you will learn more about Senior Pastor Tommy Twitty online at www.trtministries.com, or at his local church website www.wodca.org.

About the Author:

Sr. Pastor Tommy R Twitty

"An anointed vessel of God,

seeking the heart of God for God's people"

A visionary, teacher, prophet, author, and founder of TRT Ministries and Reaching Outside the Walls Ministry (ROTW). He is a native of Chesnee, South Carolina, and the Senior Pastor of Word of Deliverance Church in Gaffney, S.C. Pastor Twitty is a devoted husband to his lovely wife, Elect Lady Nicole Humphries Twitty, and father to their three beautiful children, Shante', Rashawn, and Amber.

The Word of Deliverance Church is a youthful, multi-cultural, soul-winning ministry, with a message of love, healing and deliverance, where "All People of All Races are Freely Welcomed." Pastor Twitty's vision is to "work diligently to build the Saints, that the Saints might build the City." The first step in the building process is to get people to understand that "if you change the way you think, you will change the way you live". With this vision in his heart, he is dedicated to "Reaching Outside The Walls" to seek out and save the lost, whatever the cost.

In 1998, God gave Pastor Twitty a vision to establish ROTW, and to write and make plain the vision as He had instructed. God told Pastor Twitty to bring both the church and the world together to become the Kingdom of Goc. The mission of ROTW Ministries is to go out into the cities, cross over into other states, travel around the world, and to other nations, to restore, deliver, and liberate God's people, that they may declare unto themselves and others that they shall live and not die in the Kingdom of God.

God revealed to Pastor Twitty what the latter days would be like if he did what he believed was godly. He told him how to bring the world into the Kingdom of God. He told him how to lead the twentieth century church from its current state, how to dress her, arm her, and to equip her, that she may lose her traditional form and her religious status. Pastor Twitty was told to prepare for both a kingdom position and a priesthood role alongside men and women of God with the same vision. The vision is to bring the body of Christ together as one, that we may go outside the walls and begin the work of the kingdom, by gathering those who are lost in the system and have gotten entangled in the snares of the system. The "system" has failed us, but the Kingdom will enable the world and the church to come together.

As founder of TRT Ministries, Pastor Twitty has authored the book *Wait for It*, which is based upon Isaiah 40:31:

> *But they that wait upon the Lord shall renew their strength; they shall mount up with wings as eagles; they shall run, and not be weary; and they shall walk, and not faint.*

This book is based upon everyday living and is backed by God's Word. Pastor Twitty has taught several leadership series, but is most proud of the series "Making of a Leader" and *"The Nehemiah Strategic Planning Manual and Study Guide"*, in which he has taken the Word of God and the things of the spirit and made them applicable to the lives of everyday people who are seeking an understanding of God's plan for their lives. Apostle-Elect Twitty has also published the book *The Answer*, which is based upon the book of Nehemiah. This book provides you with answers to the questions for which you continue to seek God, as they relate to building your life, ministry, career, and business. Most recently, Apostle-Elect Twitty completed *The Revelation of Jesus, Characteristics of the Seven Churches*, a dynamic book for learning about the seven churches of Asia Minor and the time in which we are living.

God has blessed Pastor Twitty to be heard on the radio and to be seen on several television shows. He is becoming more and more involved in his role in the communities, as he expands the ROTW program, **Bridging the Gap**. In spite of all that Pastor Twitty has accomplished, he always, without hesitation or reservation, gives God the glory, because he knows that nobody but God could have opened the doors that have been opened for him.

www.ingramcontent.com/pod-product-compliance
Lightning Source LLC
LaVergne TN
LVHW021342080426
835508LV00020B/2072